COUPLED
FOR LIFE

Overcoming Personality Differences in Marriage

BEYOND TWO
Know Yourself - Change Your Future!

Advanced Certified
Personality Trainer

Karen C. Ward

Beyond Two Publishing

Coupled For Life – Overcoming Personality Differences in Marriage

© 2019 by Karen Ward

Visit http://www.beyondtwollc.com

Requests for information should be addressed to:

Beyond Two Publishing, P.O. Box 44592, Fort Washington, MD 20749

ISBN-13: 978-1-7340528-1-7

Cover Design: Michael_grx

Interior Design: Alexey Zgola

Printed in the United States of America

Dedication

This book is dedicated to the love of my life.

From the time I laid eyes on him, I knew he was the one. He was the one to whom I would be "Coupled for Life". Years ago at a company cook-out, I introduced him as the love of my life and he is indeed that for me. He is not perfect, but guess what, neither am I. I want to thank the hardest working man in the world and the love of my life who has supported me emotionally and financially while I pursue my dreams.

I know this book will bring about healing for many other couples because you said "yes" to sharing our story.

Danzel E. Ward, I LOVE YOU TO LIFE!

Acknowledgments

Thank you!

Above all, I want to give thanks to my Lord and Savior Jesus Christ who has a mighty plan for my life. As I was writing the charter for my business and detailing what Beyond Two would offer, I heard the Holy Spirit say, "And Books". This book is the first installment of the promises of God!

I want to thank my amazing children (Danzell, Shante', Brianna, and Aloris) who see me in ways no one else can, as an overcomer, a finisher and through the eyes of unconditional love. My three beautiful granddaughters (Katherine, L'oriel, and Morgan) who I want to pass the legacy of knowing you can be everything you dream you can be, at any age. Thanks to my new gifts that my deceased nephew Everett Corley left behind his daughter Addison and her mom Na-Keshia Rawlings.

To my siblings (Marie Pannell, Connie Wilson, Leo Wilson, Denise Beaty, Renee Godfrey, and Kirk Wilson) who love and support me in all I do. You are some of my biggest cheerleaders.

Special Acknowledgments

Much love to Shadonna Gibson, Celeste Owens and Sundra Ryce who have coached, encouraged and pushed me into my purpose.

Great appreciation to my Elite 13 sisters (Celeste Owens, LaToya

Fonville, Chereace Richards, Cozzette Lyons-Jones, Chanelle Mann, Janelle Briscoe, Nichole Thomas, Omiana Muller, Sundra Ryce, Tyra Kingsland, Cherise Folkes) who prayed for me and supported the vision that God gave me to become a writer.

To each of the person who contributed to this book by sharing your incredible testimonies (My husband Danzel, Anthony & Angela, Stan & Chereace, Andel & Celeste, Vince & Joy, Jon & Mary, Frank & Stephanie) I am forever indebted to you for sharing your hearts with us and providing hope to the readers of Coupled For Life.

Special thanks to Pastor Deborah Evans, my mentor, and friend, who introduced me to "Personality Plus" by Florence Littauer and who has been a constant source of encouragement and advice.

There are no words to truly express my gratitude to Shadonna Gibson, Connie Wilson and Cynthia Lewis who painstakingly edited and contributed to the content of this book. I am forever in your debt.

I love you all!

Table of Contents

The Prelude

Introduction

While sitting in our marriage counselor's office, I was talking about something that upset me, and at the end of my sentence my husband exclaimed, "See, she thinks she's my mother." I stood up, grabbed my purse and responded, "Stick a fork in me, I'm done!" At that moment, for me, our marriage was over. The counselor leaped to his feet, stood in front of me, and said: "Calm down everybody and sit down." As I sat down, I began shaking my legs, something I did when I was angry, to calm myself down.

My husband saw me as (s)mothering and I saw him as childish. What we could not see was our personality differences were preventing us from understanding and relating to each other.

The counselor said my husband and I needed to put God in the center of our marriage. He said, "When God is in the center of your marriage, as you grow closer to Him, you will grow closer to one another." At that moment God was speaking to me. I knew the key to restoring my marriage was understanding each other's personality and surrendering my will for God's will, even when I did not want to. I understood that this was not the end of our marriage, but that it was the end of our major misunderstandings. And that led us to explore each other's personality differences. The Bible states *"So then, they are no longer two but one flesh. Therefore, what God has joined together, let not man separate."* (Matthew 19:6). Then I realized God wanted us Coupled for life!

Who did you marry? Most of us believe we know our mates, but then we discover we do not. We think they are bossy, frivolous with money, hyper-sensitive or appear to be a slacker. So, what do we do next? If you said, "Try to fix them," that's what most people attempt to do. Often, we try to change our mates into our vision of the perfect person. Trying to change your mate doesn't work because one of you, if not both of you will be unhappy. Some of the characteristics we try to change about our mate stem from the root of their personality.

Since we are born with our personalities and our life experiences shape us, we view people and our relationships through that lens.

One reason I wrote this book is to help couples recognize their personality strengths and their weaknesses, and how to understand them. My desire, much like that of the Lord's, is that married people, stay "Coupled for Life" (C4L). It took me many years to understand that my husband is not like me, he does not think or act like me. Although we share similar personality styles, there are distinctions in our strengths, weaknesses, and our upbringings. Therefore, the way we see and react to situations often differ. Because my husband and I did not understand each other's personality styles, it caused a great deal of strife in our relationship. I learned that my strong, assertive, and disorganized personality traits proved challenging for my husband and others. My husband's authoritative, action-oriented, and my way or the highway personality traits caused me to respond in ways that dishonored the Lord.

The Lord expects honorable companionship between couples, which means communication is an essential tool and each must clarify their needs with care and concern. To do this, it is important to understand how God created us and how He plans to use our personality styles in our relationships to develop stronger and healthier marriages. According to the Bible, [1 Peter 3:7], husbands are urged to *"live with their wives and treat them with understanding."* This means husbands must seek to understand. The role of wives is to help their husbands to understand them. Therefore, it is imperative we understand that God created our unique personalities; He desires to use them to help us to develop stronger, healthier relationships.

Understanding and applying personality strategies is a calling that the Lord placed on my life. Learning to appreciate personality differences in my marriage required me to surrender my will and my way for God's perfect will for me. Please understand this did not happen because I wanted it to happen. It happened because the Lord required my submission and I was obedient. Although it has been a journey, both my husband and I recognize that unification and reconciliation between spouses are God's desire for our marriage. This is true for all marriages and we honor God by how we honor our spouses.

Other reasons for this book are to help you see that change starts with you and not with changing your spouse. It is to show you there is hope in all marital challenges. I pray this book helps you to overcome personality differences and encourages you to stay "Coupled for Life."

I was speaking to a millennial who was planning to marry in a few months. I asked her what advice she would like from a book about staying "Coupled For Life." Her first answer was, "The best way to handle conflict." The second thing was, "When to say when." I said, "What does that mean?" She said, "When it's time to give up and get a divorce." This got me thinking about her question since I asked her about staying "Coupled for Life." Sometimes when couples get married, they are not always thinking about reaching the place in the vows that states, "Until death do us part." Instead, they look for a loophole in the marriage contract to serve as an insurance policy to exit the marriage if things do not work out. The unfortunate thing is that couples who plan to have a divorce option, jump ship before they give their marriage a fighting chance. What they don't take into consideration is that "everything changes, nothing stays the same." Our feelings should show when something is wrong, but not be used as a final decision-maker. How we feel today, we won't feel in two days, two weeks, two months or two years from now. A hasty decision to break up happens because we misunderstand our mate's personality, trust our unreliable feelings and not God.

Another reason marriages fail is because of our expectations. My mate does not understand me, does not listen to me, does not want this as much as I do, etc. When we expect people to do and say what we want, it will lead to disappointment. Enough of these situations can cause dissension in the marriage between the couple. Do you understand your personality? Do you understand your spouse's personality? Let's explore them.

Chapter 1
The Premise

Personality Overview

When I met Dan, my husband, one thing that attracted me to him was his sense of humor and adventurous side. He makes life seem like fun and is fearless in his approach to it. He took me on a lot of exciting adventures and I enjoyed experiencing new things with him. I remember we took a twelve-hour road trip in which I drove more than half the way. I would have never considered driving that distance prior to meeting him. I was excited to experience these things with him. Because of my upbringing, I was timid about trying new things. My mother was a very cautious person and, because of that, she made me question my spontaneous nature and sense of adventure. I was afraid to explore the world because I let the fear of the unknown grip me and keep me from experiencing life to the fullest. Dan made me believe I could do anything. My personality is fun-loving and adventurous. Typically, I am a risk-taker, but that was greatly influenced by my upbringing.

There are studies that show that we are born with our personalities. If you pay close attention to little babies, you can see their personality traits emerge. Understanding how our personalities impact our decisions and how we treat one another is important in creating successful relationships. Our personality traits can either enhance our relationship or destroy it.

During several of my speaking engagements, some of my clients would say things like, "I was born bossy" or "loud" or "judgmental" or "sarcastic." Although it is important to identify our weaknesses, that does not give us a pass to operate in them. We should make every attempt to surrender our weaknesses to God and seek to change the behavior(s). One of my favorite scriptures is in Psalms 51:10, *"Create in me a clean heart, O God; and renew a right spirit within me."* To understand what personality traits we need to change, we must first understand "The Personalities."

The Personalities

I was a member of Victorious Living Now Ministries, an adult women's mentoring program, headed by my friend and mentor Pastor Deborah Evans, where she facilitated face-to-face mentoring and training sessions. One year, she offered a book of the month that she would teach from and we would explore together the spiritual implications. One book we read was "Personality Plus" by Florence Littauer. I always wondered why people acted the way they acted and I wanted to learn more about it. If I am being honest, it offended me when I read that my personality style was self-centered. I didn't see that as my character flaw until I thought about my personality as a young person. I realized that I would monopolize conversations and was only interested in what I wanted to talk about. I did not see that as a personality flaw; however, my relationship with God caused me to change my view and behavior.

Anyway, I was more intrigued than ever to learn more about "The Personalities." After looking into "The Personalities" further and going through the required training, I became a Certified Personality Trainer (CPT) and Speaker and later, became a lifetime Advanced Certified Personality Trainer and Speaker. Learning about "The Personalities" has given me a new perspective on my relationships with my husband and people in general. Understanding "The Personalities" has taught me not to judge others because of our differences, but to appreciate our differences.

Personality Styles

During the dating, engagement, and marriage stages, we do not always take into consideration each other's personality traits. Each of us has personality quirks that can endear or aggravate. Our mate's positive traits draw us to them, but we don't take the time to understand their personality weaknesses. Understanding each other's personality styles helps to strengthen our relationships. To identify your personality style, take the personality profile test in the Appendix of this book.

Let's examine personality styles as it relates to marriage, but first, let's learn about "The Personalities" as follows:

There are many schools of thought regarding personality theories. As an Advanced Certified Personality Trainer, I wrote this book using the personality trait theory, "The Personalities," developed by Florence Littauer. The Personalities explain personality styles basic desires, emotional needs, strengths, and weaknesses.

There are four personality styles; most of us operate predominantly in what are our primary and secondary styles. The Personalities comprise of two extraverted and two introverted personality styles. An extraverted personality gets energy by being around people and an introverted personality gets energy from within. You could possess both extraverted styles (primary and secondary), both introverted styles or one extraverted and one introverted style. As you learn about the characteristics of each personality style, you may identify with most of the traits of your personality style. However, some may not apply to you. Most people do not possess every characteristic of a personality style because of their unique weaknesses, strengths, upbringing, and experiences. Some people gain some of their personality styles traits because of learned behavior. For instance, my mother was an introverted personality style, who need things in order. She hated when we would go into cabinets and closets and leave the doors open. My personality style would not notice that the doors were opened or closed because it is unimportant to me. However, I learned that from my mother and now get irritated when I see someone leave a cabinet or closet door open. Had I not witnessed that during my childhood, I probably wouldn't have developed a pet peeve about people leaving cabinets or doors open. Therefore, it is important to understand each of the four personality styles, Sanguine, Choleric, Melancholy, and Phlegmatic to understand ourselves and others.

Let's look at the Brassy Sanguine.

The Brassy Sanguine

The strengths of the Brassy Sanguine includes being popular, outgoing, fearless, and funny. They are social butterflies, who are a bold and fun-loving personality style. When a Sanguine meets you for the first time, they will talk to you as if they have known you all of their lives. They enjoy living life to the fullest with reckless abandon. Sanguines are spontaneous and like trying new and exciting things, for instance, bungee jumping, ziplining, jet-skiing, etc.

In relationships, they make life fun because they love entertaining and hanging out with friends and family. They have a good sense of humor and are practical jokers. Because they stay in the present, they are not interested in developing long-range plans, a weakness for this personality style. Sanguines are frivolous with money and look at the budget as a restriction versus a necessity.

My primary personality style is Sanguine, which is my husband's secondary personality style. We love to travel, shop, eat, drink, and be merry. We enjoy entertaining and spending time with family and friends. I remember when we purchased our home, we did so by making sure we had a house that could accommodate our fun-filled lifestyle. One flaw of a Sanguine is that we do not always take into consideration what others might need or want. One of our daughters is an introvert and she hated that we had so many parties. She felt obligated to hug, kiss, and speak to every family member and/or friend. To expect an introvert to interact with a lot of people is unrealistic and drains their energy. Sanguines are also very talkative and need to fill the air with noise. They tell very interesting stories, but rarely give others an opportunity to speak or voice their opinions.

I am a Sanguine personality. In the past, I was very forgetful and would miss deadlines and appointments. I have left drinks on the top of my car and driven off with it spilling everywhere. Then there have been times when I have driven my husband's car, parked it in the parking lot and forgot I drove it, causing me to run around looking for my car before I remembered I drove his car. Having a different personality style, my husband certainly didn't understand how I could forget which car I drove.

The Choleric personality is by nature, the Commander-in-Chief; let's explore this in more detail.

The Commander-in-Chief Choleric

The Commander-in-Chief Choleric personality strengths, they are strong leaders who are decisive and strategic thinkers. They can run just about anything they desire; businesses, organizations, projects, etc. The Choleric is social; however, they differ from the Sanguine because the Choleric socializes with a purpose in mind. Cholerics socialize for networking opportunities and not to make friends or be friendly. Choleric personalities have great ideas and execute them with ease.

However, their weaknesses are that they can also be very controlling, bossy, and abrasive in their communications. They have their little need for friends and therefore do not connect with people on a personal level unless they see a benefit. In relationships, the Choleric have clear personal, professional, and spiritual goals and when they marry, it is until death. This personality style needs to carve out sufficient time for their mates because their primary focus is on working and climbing the ladder of success. They are power-hungry and can find themselves in get-rich schemes if they are not careful.

My husband, the Commander-in-Chief Choleric, has always been a take-charge, get it done, person. He operates with a "my way or the highway" mentality because he believes he knows the best outcome of any situation. He is always fixing problems for anyone who presents him with a challenge.

If the Choleric is not careful they will become overbearing in relationships. Because the Choleric is a fixer, they can get too involved in the lives of other people. As a spouse, they tell their spouse what to do, when to do it, where to do it, and how to do it. They believe that if they don't give their spouse instructions on what to do, they will not figure it out on their own. The Commander-in-Chief Choleric can certainly take compassion lessons from the Melancholy.

Next, the Methodical Melancholy.

The Methodical Melancholy

The Methodical Melancholy personality style's strengths are compassionate, serious-minded, and intelligent people. Melancholies live with a structured and scheduled agenda. They have organized and impeccable living spaces. They believe "everything has a place and everything needs to be in its place." Unless there is a life event, for instance, divorce, job loss, etc., Melancholies have high credit scores. Financial management is important to them. They have a logical approach to any situation. They are cautious with whom they give money or how they invest. Melancholy people keep track of their money and they know how much money they have down to the penny.

Because of their weaknesses, Melancholies do not easily trust people, they are suspicious of others and keep their circle of friends small. They are also prone to depression because of their high expectations of themselves and others.

In relationships, they are critical of their mates. They expect them to have a life plan and to follow it to the letter. They want their mates to be smart with how they manage their resources and financially secure. They enjoy doing things that improve the mind, such as, going to museums, historical sites, and educational movies.

My best friend is a Melancholy personality. I will not go on a double date to the movies with her and her husband because they like educational or historical movies. My husband and I like comedies or action movies and have little desire to see educational or historical types of movies. Melancholies have nice possessions and dislike other people destroying them. When you come into their house, expect to remove your shoes and treat their property better than you treat your own. Although, both The Methodical Melancholy and the Peaceful Phlegmatic are intraverted personality styles.

Now, let's talk about the Peaceful Phlegmatic

The Peaceful Phlegmatic

Strengths of the Peaceful Phlegmatic personality styles are nice, loyal, and a calming force. When the world is in an uproar, the Phlegmatic is a quiet reassuring person who believes that no matter what you are going through, everything will be okay. They are good friends and listeners who will keep your confidence high. I always say that every family needs a Phlegmatic person. They bring a calming spirit to their environment.

The Phlegmatic personality weaknesses present as if they are uninvolved in what is going on in the world around them, especially if it does not directly impact them. They appear to be lazy because they are always lying down or taking naps. Phlegmatics show very little enthusiasm or emotions and has a blank look on their face that is difficult to decipher.

In a relationship, the Phlegmatic is non-confrontational and prefers to stay at home. If they go out, they prefer to be around small groups of people. They will stay married unless the marriage becomes too contentious or their mates pursue a divorce. I have a friend whose husband is a Phlegmatic. Whenever we get together, he has very little to say. He grunts to signify agreement.

Chapter 2

The Purpose

Personality and Marriage

Marriage is God's first covenant; therefore, it is important to Him. What do you think God is thinking when we trivialize marriage? When we give up too soon? About the alarming rate of divorce? The answer is in this scripture that states, *"For the Lord God of Israel says That He hates divorce..."* Malachi 2:16.

Let's examine recent divorce statistics compiled by Wilkinson & Finkbeiner, ATTYS from various sources. Researchers estimate that:

▸ Every 13 seconds, there is one divorce in America.

▸ 50 percent of all marriages in the United States will end in divorce or separation.

▸ 41 percent of all first marriages end in divorce.

▸ 60 percent of second marriages end in divorce.

▸ 73 percent of all third marriages end in divorce.

▸ The United States has the 6th highest divorce rate in the world

With statistics like these, many couples use divorce to resolve their relationship problems. In case you missed the memo, "MARRIAGE IS HARD WORK," but if you stay the course, it's worth it. If for one minute you believe Satan will leave your marriage alone, you are wrong. He will throw everything at you and your spouse to get you to abandon your covenant relationship. You may have noticed that I used the word covenant instead of a contract and there is a reason I did. According to Upcounsel, *"The difference between a marriage contract and a marriage covenant is a contract is invalid when one of the involved parties violates it. On the other hand, a covenant remains intact even if one of the parties breaches it. The covenant is based on your values and is honored even if the other person does not fulfill their pledge to it."* If you give up on your covenant marriage, you will miss the beauty of what God intended for it.

I can tell you that there were many times when I wanted to throw in the towel, citing reasons like; *"he gets on my nerves," "he doesn't understand me," "he does what he wants without any consideration for me or our family," "he doesn't listen to anything I say,"* and *"I don't trust him to do the right thing."* Anyone of these reasons causes some couples to head to a divorce lawyer.

Our personality drives every decision that we make, especially as it pertains to relationships. It also impacts how we communicate with and relate to one another, manage our money, spend our time, raise our children, express love, etc. Each personality style views marriage in its own unique way and our beliefs are partially shaped by them. Relationships can be challenging enough when we understand one another, but very difficult when we do not.

I remember hearing the statement "My perspective is my reality." Well if that's the case, we need to examine our perspectives to understand how this is impacting our relationships. How we see each other matters.

How We See Each Other

Scriptures: *"And why do you look at the speck in your brother's eye, but do not consider the plank in your own eye? 4 Or how can you say to your brother, 'Let me remove the speck from your eye'; look, a plank is in your own eye? 5 Hypocrite! First, remove the plank from your own eye, and then you will see clearly to remove the speck from your brother's eye".* (Matthew 7:3-5)

The way we see each other is also linked to our personalities. Understanding why we see each other as we do can help us to be less judgmental and more appreciative of our mate's differences, as stated in Matthew 7:3-5.

The chart below outlines how each personality views their own and other personality styles' strengths and weaknesses.

How We See Each Other

Views		Sanguine	Choleric	Melancholy	Phlegmatic
Sanguine	Strengths	Dynamic	Bold	Profound	Kind
	Weakness	Annoying	Know-it-all	Stand-offish	Uninvolved
Choleric	Strengths	Engaging	Powerful	Intelligent	Dependable
	Weakness	Unproductive	Aggressive	Complainer	Lazy
Melancholy	Strengths	Amusing	Daring	Forward-thinking	Loyal
	Weakness	Immature	Abrasive	Undeserving	Lacks Initiative
Phlegmatic	Strengths	Exciting	Doer	Knowledgeable	Calm
	Weakness	Loud	Demanding	Picky	Afraid

Source: Karen Ward ~ ACPS

The Sanguine Viewpoint

The Sanguine views other Sanguine personalities, operating in their strengths as a dynamic, engaging and having the time of their lives. In their weaknesses, they see other Sanguines as obnoxious, loud, and always showing off to get attention. They are self-centered and will monopolize and refocus conversations onto themselves.

When I see another Sanguine speaker, I admire their boldness and entertaining style of communicating. There were times when I envied the ease in how they drew an audience into their stories. However, I realized over the years, that other Sanguine personalities were annoying to me and for some of the same reasons they annoyed other personalities. They are limelight stealers, very loud, and have no filter with what they say to people. Although they can be very funny, they are not as funny when their jokes are pointed at other Sanguines.

The Sanguine views Choleric strengths as people who are bold and highly accomplished in all their endeavors. They see the Choleric personality weaknesses as a know-it-all and confrontational in how they communicate and deal with others. The Choleric is exciting to watch because they jump into projects with no fear of failure. However, thinking they are always right causes the Sanguine to second guess themselves.

Sanguines view the Melancholy personality operating in their strengths as a deep and intellectual thinker. In their weaknesses, they see the Melancholy as distant and suspicious of others. Sanguine personalities love engaging with Melancholies because they evoke deep thought and consideration on a topic. However, they feel judged by Melancholies because they are always correcting their grammar, ideals, and perspectives.

Sanguines sees the Phlegmatic personality, in their strengths, as sweet, kind, and non-confrontational. However, in their weaknesses, they view Phlegmatics as uninvolved people who are unconcerned with the world around them. Due to the Phlegmatic quiet, non-confrontational demeanor, Sanguines love being around Phlegmatics because they have a captive audience at all times. However, the Sanguine is annoyed when the Phlegmatic will not co-sign their point of view or will not get involved with the Sanguine's many activities.

In relationships, Sanguines can be viewed as exciting, fun, irresponsible, and obnoxious. As a Sanguine, I try to go to every event I am invited to and would get angry if my husband does not want to go with me.

The Choleric Viewpoint

The Choleric sees the Sanguine in their strengths as a charmer and able to capture the attention of others. Although, in their weaknesses, they appear to waste a lot of time and have a poor follow-up to commitments. The Choleric loves to see a Sanguine work a room because of their ability to make good networking connections with people. However, they think that Sanguines spend too much time talking about nothing and not being productive.

The Choleric sees other Choleric personalities in their strengths as a powerful force and a mover and a shaker. However, in their weaknesses, they see them as very aggressive with a negative attitude. Cholerics admire other Cholerics drive and determination to succeed. However, they don't like to be controlled by anyone, especially another Choleric whose ideals they don't share.

The Choleric sees the Melancholy, in their strengths, as intelligent and purposeful in their approach to everything. However, the Choleric views the Melancholy, in their weaknesses, as complainers, highly critical of others and slow-moving. The Choleric appreciates the Melancholy's ability to look at an idea from every angle and consider its impact on everyone. However, the Choleric is a mover and a shaker and believes everyone should move at a rapid pace. Otherwise, they are just wasting time. The Melancholy's slow and methodical thought process slows the pace of getting things accomplished which aggravates the Choleric.

The Choleric sees the Phlegmatic as someone they can count on and is supportive. The Choleric sees the Phlegmatic weaknesses as lazy and uninvolved in the cares of the world. The Choleric likes being around a Phlegmatic because they are supportive and yield decisions to the Choleric. Although, the Choleric Phlegmatic's indecisiveness serves as a source of frustration to the Choleric.

In relationships, Choleric personality can be viewed as powerful, decisive, controlling, and always right. My Choleric friend is always right about everything, at least he/she thinks he/she is. A spouse who always thinks they are right can be annoying to their mate because, even if they are wrong, they can make you feel as though they are right.

The Melancholy Viewpoint

The Melancholy views the Sanguine, in their strengths, as uninhibited, amusing, and fun to be around. However, they see the Sanguine personality, in their weaknesses, as child-like with loose lips.

The Melancholy sees the Choleric personality as bold and daring in their decisions and actions. However, the Melancholy sees the Choleric, in their weaknesses, as abrasive and rude in how they communicate.

Melancholy people see other Melancholy personality styles as smart, forward-thinking and self-reflective. However, they see their weaknesses as critical and judgmental.

The Melancholy personality sees Phlegmatic personalities, in their strengths, as calm and a good listener. However, they see the Phlegmatic weaknesses as hesitant and lacking initiative.

The Melancholy, in relationships, can be viewed as profound, compassionate, critical and a complainer. I have a lot of Melancholy friends and family members. They complain about their spouses, using the premise that they are just trying to better understand them.

The Phlegmatic Viewpoint

The Phlegmatic views the Sanguine, in their strengths, as exciting and living life to the fullest, but sees their weaknesses as loud and over-the-top.

The Phlegmatic sees the Choleric as a doer and fearless, but their weaknesses as demanding and aggressive.

The Phlegmatic sees the Melancholy as knowledgeable and directed, but their weaknesses as picky and critical of them.

The Phlegmatic sees the other Phlegmatic personality styles as calm and relaxed, but their weaknesses as fearful and sarcastic.

The Phlegmatic in relationships can be viewed as kind, supportive, uninvolved and disinterested in others' affairs. A Phlegmatic friend of mine annoys their spouse by making snarky remarks under their breath.

The four personality styles and viewpoints are important to understand because it allows us to recognize why we see others the way we do. And, it provides a gateway to examining "The Personalities" and our Wedding Vows.

Chapter 3

The Pact

Personalities and Wedding Vows

Scrioture: *"Therefore what God has joined together, let no one separate"* (Mark 10:9)

The upcoming chapters seek to uncover the personalities and how each of them views and behaves in marriage from the perspective of a traditional wedding vow. Let's first examine what threatens our marriages:

"Statistically, there are 9 divorces in the time it takes for a couple to recite their wedding vows (2 minutes)." When I saw this statistic, I was astounded that by the time you say I do, nine other couples are saying I don't.

In preparation for marriage, most of us tend to either use traditional wedding vows or create original ones. An example of a traditional wedding vow is *"I, (name), take thee, (name), to be my wedded husband/wife, to have and to hold, from this day forward, for better, for worse, for richer, for poorer, in sickness and in health, to love and to cherish, till death do us part, according to God's holy ordinance; and thereto I pledge thee my faith [or] pledge myself to you."* We are using this traditional wedding vow for the purposes of examining the relationship between personality and marriage vows.

Wedding vows are significant because they speak to the couple's intentions and promises to one another. When we recite our wedding vows to each other, at that time, I believe we really mean what we are saying. However, situations come up in our marriage that challenge our commitment to our vows and to each other. We view these challenges through the lens of our personalities because they impact every decision that we make and how we interpret situations. As a result, some of us take our wedding vows seriously and others of us recite them as ceremonial rituals, never to be thought of again. How you interpret your vows will dictate how you operate within your marriage. Divorce is convenient, but the Promise is not and it requires work, commitment, and resilience because it is the Pact.

Let's look at a traditional wedding vow and our personalities.

Personality and "To Have and To Hold & Leave and Cleave"

What does "to have and to hold" mean in the marriage vow? When I conducted research, I found very little information on the topic. So, I contacted my Pastor friends to get clarity on the subject. My mentor, Pastor Deborah Evans, and Minister Vince & Joy Briscoe said that this vow means:

(1) that you should learn as much about your potential spouse prior to marriage and

(2) that you should have reconciled past hurts and have taken control of your life, *"To have"* means to take, receive, and accept your spouse just the way they are. *"To hold"* is to protect and love your spouse unconditionally and passionately. This verse goes onto say, "From this day forth" that means you agree to stay "Coupled for Life" until death.

The Pastors also indicated that some officiants add *"To Leave and To Cleave"* to the traditional wedding vows. Therefore, I decided to add it to this chapter because it is another area in the relationship where couples struggle in their marriage. "To Leave and To Cleave" means to separate from your family and become one with your spouse.

Let's take a look at "To Have and To Hold" and "To Leave and To Cleave" as it relates to the Personalities.

To Have and To Hold

We all want to feel unconditionally accepted for who we are, protected and loved. We seek this from our spouses. But when they can't deliver, we will look for solutions elsewhere. We focus on our spouse's faults and try to get them to change, but get angry when they concentrate on ours. The bible states, "And above all things have fervent love for one another, for "love will cover a multitude of sins." 1 Peter 4:8. Instead of changing our spouse we should seek to love and understand them. When we do that, we won't mind covering their indiscretions. Applying knowledge of our personalities fosters love, respect, and willingness to see your spouse through the eyes of God.

The Sanguine demonstrates and professes love easily to their mate. They are very affectionate and touchy-feely. Sanguines will tell anyone, how they feel about their spouse, whether good or bad. The Sanguine does not have a filter from their brain to their mouth and therefore will talk about their spouse to or in front of others. The bible states in Proverbs 17:9, *"He who covers a transgression seeks love, But he who repeats a matter separates friends."*

> Solution: The Sanguine needs to be careful to keep their spouse's mistakes private unless mutually agreed upon. Bringing people into the marriage, unless they are professional counselors, will only cause distrust and further discord. Discuss issues with your spouse and/or seek help from a professional who will not judge you and will keep your confidence.

The Choleric is a protector by design and will do it at all costs. They want to be accepted for who they are, but they struggle to give their spouse the same consideration. The Choleric is quick to point out their spouse's flaws and then tell them they need to change. Cholerics tell you their true feelings, but not in a loving way. What benefit is the truth if it destroys your spouse.

> S o l u t i o n : The Choleric needs to recognize that there is more than one way of doing things and to yield to their spouse by compromising. When discussing an issue, the Choleric needs to soften their tone and ask open-ended questions, instead of making definitive statements. Scripture states in Proverbs 15:1, "A soft answer turns away wrath, but a harsh word stirs up anger."

The Melancholy is self-aware and they seek to learn everything about their spouse. They are compassionate and thoughtful. However, they are critical and have high expectations for their mates. They struggle with seeing every mistake their spouse makes. If not careful, the Melancholy will become a nag or will manipulate their spouses to get their way.

> S o l u t i o n : The Melancholy needs to recognize that their spouse will never meet or exceed their high expectations. They need to allow their spouses to make mistakes without the fear of judgment.

The Phlegmatic is a kind and gentle personality. They will keep their negative feelings to themselves. They can be sarcastic, which can make the spouse question their value in the relationship.

> S o l u t i o n : The Phlegmatic needs to open up and share their feelings with their spouse, without sarcasm. This shows their spouse that they care about their feelings.

Remember, *"To Have"* is your unconditional acceptance of your spouse. And, *"To Hold"* is your prized treasure (your spouse) to cherish, value, and protect. The second part of this vow is *"To Leave and To Cleave"* which deals with how we become as one with our spouse, forsaking all others (family/friends/foes).

To Leave and To Cleave

Scripture: *"Therefore a man shall leave his father and mother and be joined to his wife, and they shall become one flesh."* Genesis 2:24

"To Leave and To Cleave" means, to choose each other first and to forsake all others (parents/family/friends, etc). This is challenging due to the deep bonds that some spouses have with their families and to leave that safety and place, and trust in a spouse is frightening. With the people you were raised by or grew up with, you know what to expect, but with a spouse, it requires lowering your expectations.

I have always studied human behavior and wondered why we behave the way we do. I love watching television shows that give me a glimpse into the lives of other couples. One of the shows is "The 90 Day Fiancé." This show depicts the lives of Americans who fall in love with people who live outside the United States. When the couples fall in love and decide to marry, they must get a K1 Visa, which requires them to get married within 90 days. If they do not get married, they must return to their country. Some of these spouses had issues leaving their family members and cleaving to their mates. The families are too involved in the lives of the new couple. The couple tells their family members about the challenges they are having with their spouse, causing the family to dislike their mate.

Some of these couples have close relationships with their parents and other family members. Having a close relationship with your family is a good thing until they demand that you choose between them and your spouse. When the spouse sides with their family against their mate, it causes dissension.

The Self-Centered Sanguine

Sanguines love spending time with family and friends. They can't imagine missing any special or family events. The Sanguine will attempt to fit every fun activity into their schedule. When they marry, they expect their spouse to be their plus one. When the spouse is not interested in going to every event they are invited to, the Sanguine becomes irritated because they feel like they are missing out on fun with family and friends. The Sanguine focuses on their own feelings, instead of understanding and accepting their mates. The bible states in Philippians 2:3-4, "Don't be selfish; don't try to impress others. Be humble, thinking of others as better than yourselves. Don't look out only for your own interests, but take an interest in others, too."

I come from a large family. My parents had ten children and we are a very close-knit family. My mother had eight siblings and my father had six; therefore, we have a large extended family as well. We had large Easter, Thanksgiving, and Christmas parties. In the earlier years of my marriage, I wanted my husband to attend all of the major holidays with my family and when he didn't, I acted like a child and sulked. My husband was an only child and wanted us to make our own traditions. I had a hard time choosing my husband's proposed plans, which caused us to argue. I didn't understand why he didn't want to come to my family's event and have fun. Once we understood each other's personality style and upbringing, we were able to comprise and rotate holidays.

The Independent Choleric

Cholerics have some trouble leaving and cleaving to their spouses. The "Leaving" for the Choleric is easier because they are independent. They find it easy to disconnect from family and start anew with their spouse. However, the Choleric has a high need to be a "fixer," which causes them to stay overly involved in the lives of extended family and friends. Although Cholerics sets boundaries in their marriage, they struggle with establishing boundaries with extended family and friends. In Genesis 2:24, the bible states, *"Therefore a man shall leave his father and his mother and hold fast to his wife, and they shall become one flesh."* When the two become one, their spouse is considered number one in the relationship.

The Critical Melancholy

When the Melancholy gets married, they plan to leave and cleave to their spouse. They set clear boundaries with extended family and friends. The Melancholy is highly critical of others and lives by a moral code and expects others to do the same. However, the Melancholy does what they believe is right in their own eyes, and therefore they will side against their spouse if they deem the spouse is wrong. This causes the spouse to feel unappreciated and unsupported. The bible states in James 5:9, *"Do not complain, brethren, against one another, so that you yourselves may not be judged; behold, the Judge is standing right at the door."*

The Disengaged Phlegmatic

During the dating process, the Phlegmatic seeks marriage or a long-lasting relationship, therefore, they will easily leave and cleave to their spouse. Once married, the Phlegmatic enjoys building a bond and deeper connection with their spouse. For the Phlegmatic, they struggle with the "To cleave" part of their vow. Phlegmatics exert a lot of energy building and fostering a deep connection, however, they do not like a clingy or pushy mate. The Phlegmatic withdraws and disengages when their mate becomes clingy or pushy.

The Profession (Testimony)

Meet Anthony and Angela D. Anthony is a primary Choleric and a secondary Sanguine personality styles and Angela is primary Phlegmatic and secondary Melancholy, which means they possess all four of the personality styles. These two met and fell in love under interesting circumstances. They have been married 26 years and after you hear their story, you will wonder how they made it.

Anthony (Choleric) and Angela (Phlegmatic) said they met because of a lie, but he knew immediately he wanted to marry her the night they met, but Angela did not feel the same way.

Angela: *Anthony was in the Air Force, I was at school at the University of South Carolina. He was roommates with my nephew. Apparently, my nephew was trying to use his car. But he told Anthony that I was interested in him. I didn't know who he was and never even heard of him. So I had to play along with my nephew and pretended I was interested in him. And when my nephew came up to see me, Anthony came with him and that's how we met. In essence, I was being used for transportation.*

Note: The Phlegmatics in Angela went along with her nephew because it was easier than opposing him. After Anthony met Angela, he told her nephew he was going to marry her. The nephew was upset with Angela because:

Anthony: *I wasn't from South Carolina or the area where they grew up. Her parents wanted her with her ex-boyfriend.*

Angela: *I am the youngest child of 12 children. I had a boyfriend who I started dating during my 10th-grade year and I dated him off and on until I met Anthony. My parents and siblings thought I was going to be with him and after meeting Anthony they thought he was arrogant.*

Note: Choleric personalities are confident in themselves and their knowledge of any topic and therefore people might view them as arrogant.

Once Anthony and Angela decided to get married, Angela told her parents:

Angela: *I left my mother a note on the refrigerator telling her we were getting married. My mother called me crying and asking, "what is this" then she said, "how could I do this."*

Anthony: *A few days later, when I came to pick her up, her mother would not let me on the property. She said to me, "You made my baby choose between me and you, and she chose you, but I am going to be alright."*

Angela: *My mother told me that if I would not marry Anthony, she would buy me a house in South Carolina and I would not have to pay for anything. She also convinced my siblings to be mad at Anthony.*

Anthony: *It was so bad that one of her siblings said they "wish I would drive off a bridge and die" while another one said, "I might not be there for the wedding, but I will be there for the divorce."*

Angela: *This was such a horrible time that when we actually got married, I blocked the whole thing out. Anthony called me and said, "let's get married on my lunch break." We went to the courthouse and it was closed for renovations. We had to go next door to the jail to get married. Men in handcuffs were yelling don't marry him, marry me. Women who were under arrest was saying, "Aww, that's so nice, they are getting married." This is not what I envisioned for my wedding. To this day, I cannot remember what I wore because I blocked it out.*

Anthony: *It took another 4-5 years before I was accepted by the family and it was worth it.*

Practical Advice

Angela: The advice I would offer couples facing similar circumstances is to focus on each other. Focusing on each other and drowning out the noise of outside influences allowed us to become one.

Anthony: When you know that your potential spouse is the one you are destined to be with, you have to risk the family connection (leave) and commit to the relationship (cleave). It brought them closer than ever. Therefore, what "To Cleave" really meant to us was to put no one (Family/ friends) before the marriage.

Overcoming Personality Differences Themes

Trust God

Trust each other

Keep the faith

Cleave/Become One

Chapter 4
The Promise

Personality and "For Better, For Worse"

"For better, for worse," by my definition, means "coupled for life." It means that You:

- ▶ will work out your problems, no matter the challenges you encounter
- ▶ manage your expectations and not force them on your spouse
- ▶ put your spouse's needs first and are not selfish

When we say *"For better or for worse"* on our wedding day, these are examples of what we really mean:

For better or for worse, if you make and keep me happy.

For better or for worse, if you do what I say.

For better or for worse, if my parents, family, or friends agree with it.

For better or for worse, if you don't get fat.

For better or for worse, if I can trust you.

For better or for worse, if you keep a job.

For better or for worse, if we separate our finances.

For better or for worse, if someone else doesn't come along that treats me better.

Unfortunately, we have unreasonable expectations of one another, some of them stemming from our personality differences.

Remember, my primary personality style is Sanguine and my secondary style is Choleric. My husband's primary is Choleric, and his secondary is Sanguine. As a Sanguine, I have an explosive temper and as a Choleric, I hold a grudge. As a Choleric, my husband is controlling and as a Sanguine, flirtatious. When he told me what to do, which was often, I got irritated. For example; my husband tells me how to pay bills when he does not monitor how much money is in our account and what bills are due and when. This was annoying because I worked as a corporate manager who managed million-dollar budgets. I couldn't understand why he thought I needed him to tell me how to pay bills. I would react with a negative tone or attitude to his budget strategies. Because of my attitude, he felt disrespected by me and because I believed, he didn't trust me to make decisions I felt unloved by him. In actuality, we didn't understand each other's personalities and how to overcome our differences.

This chapter was the most challenging one for me to write. My husband and I went through the worst part of the *"for better, for worse"* vow in our marriage. For me, this part of our wedding vows is where I learned to walk out my faith. I don't want to mislead you into thinking that this is the only vow that challenged us. During our 25 years of marriage, we experienced challenges in almost each one of these traditional wedding vows. However, this is the one that I believe had the biggest impact on our relationship. Because we fought to overcome these challenges, I feel I can confidently write this book and share our story. It is my prayer that our testimony will give you hope that God can restore and redeem any relationship. Scriptures state, in Revelations 12:11, *"And they overcame him because of the blood of the Lamb and because of the word of their testimony, and they did not love their life even when faced with death."* Our testimonies are the keys to unlocking the hope to stay committed to the relationship.

Every relationship goes through difficult times. Challenges could range from, trust issues (lying, cheating, or mishandling finances, etc.), substance abuse (drugs or alcohol), or addictive behaviors (pornography, gambling, or sex addiction, etc.). These issues can lead to a divorce, but it does not have to end that way. God wants us to have reconciled and unified relationships. The bible states in 1 Corinthians 7:10-11, *"To the married I give this charge (not I, but the Lord): the wife should not separate from her husband (but if she does, she should remain unmarried or else be reconciled to her husband), and the husband should not divorce his wife."* Clearly, this scripture demonstrates that God wants us to be "Coupled for Life." However, the choice is ours to make. God will not force us (His permissive will) to stay married, but when we seek to please Him, we should make every effort to do His will. When you choose to please Him, God will give you (His perfect will) amazing grace to get through troubled times in your marriage.

Before I delve into my experience with "For Better, For Worse," let's discuss each personality style and this wedding vow:

For Better - The Forgive and Forget Sanguine

When the Sanguine is operating in their strengths, they are fun to be around. They enjoy life to the fullest and want everyone around them to have fun. Even when they get angry, they quickly get over it because they don't want tension in the relationship. Although the Sanguine can easily get over an argument they assume others can as well, which is not always true. They prefer to forgive and forget the transgressions of their mate and get back to happier times. They like seeing the best in their spouses and avoiding arguments. Sanguine people will ignore obvious signs that something is wrong. They look at life through rose-colored glasses and are likely to sweep issues under the rug before they are resolved, thus running the risk of their issues repeating themselves.

For Worse - The Stubborn Sanguine

As previously stated, Sanguine personalities do not like dealing with difficult situations. Also, they are quick-tempered and do not tolerate nonsense from anyone, especially their mate. They are emotional and overreact to hurtful situations. Sanguines believe the louder they are, the more they are heard and understood; however, this only makes them loud and misunderstood. Their mates will either tune them out or shut down during the disagreement.

In relationships, when Sanguines are faced with difficult situations, they make their feelings known, leave the relationship and cut their losses. Sanguines will end the marriage and move onto the next one to avoid being unhappy. Because the Sanguine desires to have fun and they have a high need to be liked, Sanguines can find themselves involved in an adulterous relationship.

"For worse" shows up for Sanguines when they are constantly told "no" for anything they want or want to do. They will order things without their spouse's knowledge, take money out of the bank to fund their fun activities, or seek someone who allows them to enjoy life without considering the consequences.

Anyone who knows me knows that I love to laugh and see the humor in any situation. I am always telling amusing stories and I like to make others laugh and have fun. However, when I got angry, I became verbally and sometimes physically abusive. During my marriage, I discovered that my husband had an affair. When I learned about his infidelity, I was so angry that my heart was beating rapidly, and I couldn't think clearly. I just remember asking him questions and when he tried to cover it up, I lashed out at him with as much venom as I could muster. Do I regret this now? Yes, I do. I wish I had controlled my anger because it only made things worse between us. Because I struggled with unforgiveness, I wanted to leave him that night and cut my losses, but I heard the Lord say, *"Be still."* Being still was the last thing I wanted to do, but I was obedient to the Lord because my desire was to please Him. I surrendered my anger and hurt feelings to God and He gave me the grace to get through that difficult time.

For Better – The Take Charge Choleric

The Choleric spouse is take-charge, hardworking, and a good provider. They are always looking for opportunities to advance their careers and secure a legacy for their family. The Choleric loves nice things and will work long hours to ensure they get what they want. They make quick and sound decisions regarding family, home life, or business activities. Because the Choleric is a natural-born leader, they assume their position as a leader at work and at home.

In relationships, the Choleric develops a strategy for running their lives efficiently and they expect their spouse and children to fall in-line without discussion or opposition.

For Worse - The Vengeful Choleric

The Choleric personality controls people by the threat of anger. If betrayed, the Choleric will lash out at you verbally and sometimes physically to make their point. The Choleric comes off as an aggressive person. When pushed or agitated, they become hostile. The Choleric must have a strategy for everything and leaves nothing to chance. They want to ensure that their plans will work out before investing time and energy in it. If their spouse cannot get on board with the plan, they get frustrated, take note of their failure to adhere to the plan and blame them if the plan doesn't work. The Choleric expects a spouse to go along with their plans because they think they are always right.

One of my clients complains that his wife agrees to a plan but changes it at the last minute. The wife felt criticized because the husband said, "We had a plan and you didn't follow through with it and now the scheduled is ruined." When the spouse changed the plan, the Choleric became rigid and abrasive in how they communicated with their mate. The spouse brings this up every time there is an argument.

When a Choleric proposes something, they are telling you what to do; it is not a suggestion. When you agree to the Choleric's plan, it becomes law and when the spouse doesn't live up to it, the Choleric will lash out in anger and hold them accountable for their broken promise.

"For worse" shows up for the Choleric when they can't control people, their environment, or when their strategy is questioned. They will develop plans with other people, not consult their spouse and expect the spouse to support their faulty decisions. If there is a financial impact, they will gamble to recoup their losses or create a get-rich-quick scheme to save face. Rather than admit their mistakes, they make up excuses to explain them away.

For Better – The Compassionate Melancholy

Melancholy is not only concerned about people they love, but they also care about people around the world. When they make decisions, they take into consideration the impact it has on others. The Melancholy does not waste time because, for them, time is a commodity. Their time is accounted for and they value their schedule and yours. They see being late as a form of disrespect. Melancholies operate on a strict schedule and live by carefully planned out goals. They don't say or do things they haven't carefully thought out. The Melancholy person has a high moral compass and expects everyone else to operate with integrity.

In relationships, the Melancholy personality style is thoughtful, remembers important dates and compassionate.

For Worse - The Unforgiving Melancholy

Melancholy personality styles are easily offended and are unforgiving. Even if you apologize, they will never forget and maybe not forgive the offense. Melancholies need a structured and scheduled marriage. They make plans well in advance and they don't handle spontaneity well. They need to consider how events and activities fit into their schedule or impact their family vision board. They plan their time and resources (money) well in advance. When their spouse wants or needs something outside of the plan, they get annoyed.

I have a client couple who are both Melancholy personality styles. They desire to have long and short-term plans, but one has it in their head, while the other desires a written plan. "One spouse says a plan that is not written, it is just a thought and thoughts are fleeting." When an issue comes up in the marriage, this spouse goes back to the lack of a written plan and the failure of the plan is the fault of the spouse who lacks one. Melancholies become depressed when plans are not in place or when they are in place and not adhered to. They do not easily forgive and will revisit the issue every time there is a conflict.

"For Worse" shows up for the Melancholy when the marriage lacks order and their carefully laid out plans are not carried out or considered. They get frustrated and will look to find a place where they can organize something. Living in a perpetual state of disorganization causes the Melancholy to fall into a depression. They will nag their spouse until they get them to agree to restore order in the marriage.

For Better – The Supportive Phlegmatic

The Phlegmatic is a supportive and caring spouse. They are easygoing and will yield to the plans of their spouse. Because the Phlegmatic is a peacemaker, they will do anything to achieve a peaceful environment. This personality is a homebody and prefers to socialize in that space. When they enter into a relationship, it is for life. They seek to form a bond early in the relationship and maintain it for the duration.

For Worse -The Nonchalant Phlegmatic

Phlegmatic people are non-confrontational and prefer not to be confronted. Phlegmatic personality styles are quiet and do not readily express themselves; however, when they do and are rejected, they are devastated. The Phlegmatic personality style is indecisive and that eventually serves as a source of frustration for their spouse. When the spouse is upset about something, the Phlegmatic's nonchalant attitude appears uncaring.

In relationships, they are supportive, kind, disinterested, and uninvolved.

I have married friends who are both Phlegmatic. They have a very laid back marriage and enjoy their personal time together. They can stay in for long periods of time and that is okay with them. They are not motivated to set long-range plans and prefer to relax instead of taking on strenuous weekend projects.

"For Worse" shows up for the Phlegmatic when they feel pushed into doing something they don't want to do. They become depressed when feeling nagged by their spouse. Phlegmatic personalities avoid conflict at all costs and retreat to a quiet sanctuary to deal with stress. To ensure they avoid future conflict, they will shut down or go along with their spouse's demands.

The Profession (Testimony)

Finding out that your marriage has been violated is devastating for a spouse especially when it involves infidelity. Hearing that my husband was cheating on me wasn't as devastating as finding out he was talking about me to her. I felt so betrayed. I dedicated my younger years with a man I felt could appreciate me. As a Sanguine, I was embarrassed and thought I was not enough for him. I also thought, what would people think once I decided to stay with him. I wanted to know everything about the affair. I am not sure I really wanted to know the answers, but I kept asking questions anyway.

As a Choleric, I wanted revenge! I wanted to publish a newspaper article to tell the world how bad he had hurt me. I wanted to physically hurt him because I did not know what to do with all my pain and anger. He really wanted to salvage the marriage because Cholerics are fixers and they seek to save the damsel in distress who happened to be me. After a lot of yelling, crying, and blaming, we decided to go to counseling. During the counseling sessions, I learned a lot about my husband that was never communicated throughout our marriage.

My husband's mother died when he was a teenager and he went to live with a great aunt. During our counseling sessions, I also learned that he had seen most of the men in his life cheat on their wives. He also had been told, after his mother died, that he would not amount to anything and that he would either end up in jail or dead. He sought to prove his family wrong. Choleric are hard workers and my husband is no exception. He worked long hours and bought us a house, cars, and anything we wanted or needed, but that could not quiet the voices that told him he was not enough. When this occurs, the Choleric will seek validation outside of the marriage.

I remember when I went to one of our counseling sessions, the counselor was asking us about our spiritual walk. In the typical boastful Sanguine way, I said I have an accountability partner, I am the head of a non-profit ministry, I am in bible study and my husband wasn't doing anything for his spiritual development. The counselor very nicely commented, "that's great that I am doing all of that, but if done with the wrong spirit it bears rotten fruit." I realized, in Choleric fashion, that I was lording my spiritual disciplines over his head. It taught me to extend grace and to recognize that because I am doing some things right, not to judge my spouse for where they are in their spiritual walk. Also, I've also learned not to be so heavenly minded that I'm no earthly good.

Note: The Choleric person believes they have the solution to every problem and that they are always right. When married to another Choleric, they feel as though they are not needed or appreciated. My husband was seeking a wife who would validate him and make him feel needed. He decided to look outside of the marriage for it. He eventually realized that his healing had nothing to do with me and it required him to heal the wounded 14-year old within.

As a Choleric wife, I realized that I was not as compassionate as I could be in our relationship. My friend, Sundra Ryce, introduced me to the idea of operating in my feminine energy. Being in my feminine energy meant that my approach to him was softer, my tone sweeter, and my behavior inviting, at least that is what it meant for me and my marriage. Choleric women are confident and self-assured which can be confused as arrogant and disrespectful. However, it is our matter-of-fact demeanor that sends the wrong signal to our mates.

Practical Advice

- ▶ During the most difficult time of our marriage, God told me to be still and I did. I did not fall victim to my emotions and God showed me that He would work miracles. One of my greatest lessons is everything changes, nothing stays the same. Given time, emotions calm and cooler heads prevail.

- ▶ I also learned to trust God that He can and will heal any marriage issue when we surrender it to Him.

- ▶ I learned that forgiveness is for me and not the other person. When we don't forgive, we become saddled with the baggage of hurt and disappointment. However, when we forgive, it frees us. Forgiveness is not easy, but it is necessary. It does not mean you let the other person off the hook, it means you let yourself off the hook of carrying around hurt feelings. Once I understood that concept and how anger crept up, I had to remind myself that if God could forgive, so could I.

Overcoming Personality Differences Themes

Trust God/Not man

Keep the faith

Forgive

Seek to understand

Chapter 5

The Provision

Personality and "For Richer, For Poorer"

"For the love of money is the root of all evil: which while some coveted after, they have erred from the faith, and pierced themselves through with many sorrows. 1Timothy 6:10

Financial hardship serves as a major source of frustration for most couples. When we are not on the same page with our finances, this leads to dissension in the relationship. Several experts believe that poor financial management is one of the major causes of divorce. Therefore, you need to understand each other's beliefs and attitudes toward money and other financial matters.

So, what does "The Personalities" have to do with managing money in marriage? The answer is a lot because each personality shapes our financial belief system and how we manage money. Most of our decisions are personality-driven and therefore understanding how each personality manages money is important. We need to develop a strategy to overcome our personality differences in money management. Let's look at each personality style as it pertains to finances and the marital relationship.

Scriptures states in 1Timothy, 6:10, *"For the love of money is a root of all kinds of evil..."*. This is a mouthful. The keywords in that scripture are *"for the love of money."* Having money is not the problem, it becomes an issue when it is the most important thing in your life. If you did a poll on the question "What is the number one reason for divorce," I think most people would say either money or communication.

The Generous Sanguine

Sanguines will give you the shirt off their backs. They will do anything to make their spouse happy. Sanguines will buy extravagant gifts and throw elaborate parties, sparing no expense. They plan trips and other exciting activities. Sanguines will spend money on their friends and pick up the tab when going out. They are free with their money and will help anyone.

Most of us have a primary (main) and secondary personality style. As stated before, I am a primary Sanguine personality. My husband is a secondary Sanguine. When we are both operating in Sanguine personality styles, we are carefree and generous in how we spend our money. We donate to charities, non-profits, or homeless people or anyone who needs our help.

Sanguine - Superficial Spender

The Sanguine personality has a sunny disposition; they could be considered a reckless optimist, reckless with their money and optimistic that everything will work out just fine. They see money as a vehicle to fund their fun excursions and to enjoy their lives to the fullest. To the Sanguine, money is no object.

Most Sanguine personality styles are frivolous with their finances. They live for the here and now and finds themselves struggling financially because of it. They spend money on the latest and greatest cars, electronics, fashion, and cosmetics, etc. They are more concerned with image than long-range goals. They are not worried about the future, because the future doesn't exist. They believe tomorrow will take care of itself.

In marriage, Sanguines can be very generous with their money, which is selfish. I know you are asking yourself, "what does that mean?" It means that Sanguines are so generous that they don't think to ask their spouse before helping people. They do not consider how helping others might impact their household finances. How the Sanguine handles money can cause a lot of stress on the marriage. Sanguines also have a high need to be liked and therefore will do anything to make people happy. They are the life of the party. They typically find themselves picking up the tab for their friends, treating them to a good meal, and entertainment. They are eager to pick up the check, even if they have to check their bank accounts first to make sure the money is in their accounts. They act as though money flows endlessly until their bank account is in the negative.

The Legacy Building Choleric

The Choleric personality is a hard worker whose desire is to provide for their family. They quickly climb the ladder of success because they have a good work ethic and they can run any business venture successfully. Their leadership skills are top-notch and they are usually the best in their field. Choleric people will ensure they have insurance policies in place to take care of their families.

The Big Spender/Risky Investor Choleric

Choleric personality styles are big spenders. They believe if you work hard, you should be able to spend your money any way you want. They also believe that accumulating big-ticket items demonstrates their level of accomplishments.

My husband has a Choleric/Sanguine personality and his philosophy is "you cannot take it with you." If the Choleric wants something and they do not have the money, they will pick up extra shifts at work or look for a part-time position. They will get what they want, even if it causes strife in their marriage, which it often does.

Choleric personalities are risky investors. They make high-risk, high reward decisions with their investments. They are willing to gamble and risk everything for a potential windfall. When they make a mistake, it is usually a big one. Their motto is "Go big or Go home."

In relationships, they make financial and investment decisions without discussing it with their spouse. This causes trouble in the household. When risky ideas fail, the Choleric will make excuses for the failed plan and quickly move onto another risky project which angers their spouse.

The Watchful Melancholy Spender

Melancholy people are good stewards of their finances. In fact, they know how much money they have down to the penny and where it is allocated. They make careful and thoughtful investments and are even more careful about loaning money to anyone.

Melancholies typically have high credit scores because they are on time with their monthly payments. They plan out their finances to ensure they can make sound purchases. A Melancholy person plans for financial difficulties by having a nest egg. However, if an unforeseen life event occurs, for example, divorce, job loss, death of a family member, etc. and if the Melancholy credit is impacted, they will tighten their grip on their finances until they recover from it. The Melancholy will work to fix their credit problems and put measures in place to ensure it never happens again.

The Miserly Melancholy Giver

Melancholy people do not trust anyone managing their money. I remember hearing Oprah Winfrey, who is clearly a Melancholy say that "you should always sign your own checks, instead of signing over control to anyone to do it for you."

The Melancholy hoards wealth and spends as little money as they can. They do not believe in loaning money unless it is for a worthy cause and they have done their research to ensure it goes to that cause. They believe if you need to ask for a loan, you must be mismanaging your own money. Therefore, why would they trust you with their money if you cannot manage your own? They also don't trust that the loan will be repaid as agreed upon.

Melancholy people like to see their money grow interest and will not touch it unless it was planned in advance or an emergency situation. They will look for other alternatives rather than risk losing a penny of their resources.

Melancholy spouses use money as a method of control. Keeping a close eye on their finances, reconciling any errors in the monthly statements and grilling their spouse on whether their purchases were sound.

If the Melancholy is not careful, they will make money or the love of money as a god.

The Conservative Phlegmatic Spender

The Phlegmatic personality is conservative in their spending because they are afraid to make the wrong decisions with money. They will save but is indecisive in how they spend money or make investments.

Because Phlegmatics are procrastinators, they will hold onto an investment longer than they should which could cost them in the long run. The Phlegmatic personality style will not discuss their finances with others. If they are having a financial problem, they usually won't convey it unless they can't avoid it. They are inclined to suffer in silence because they do not want to be confronted or judged.

The Procrastinating Phlegmatic Payer

Phlegmatic personalities are procrastinators and will not do anything that requires work. They are frugal with their money and will not spend money easily, especially on themselves. They will keep their personal property well after it's life-cycle and wear clothes and shoes until they are worn out. They consider worn-out clothes, comfy clothes.

Phlegmatic people are likely to pay late charges because of missed payment dates and have their utilities turned off.

Managing money is a challenge that most of us struggle with from time to time. Understanding what drives couples' financial decisions gives us the tools to be able to overcome these challenges.

The Profession (Testimony)

I introduce you to Stan and Chereace R. Stan is a primary Sanguine and has a secondary Choleric personality style. Chereace is a primary Choleric and has a secondary Melancholy personality style. They have been married for 19 years. Stan and Chereace met transacting business; Stan sold her tickets to an event.

Stan: *"I tell you when I gave her the two tickets I thought, and this was the God's honest truth, she is the most beautiful woman I have seen in my life, she took my breath away."*

Chereace: When I met Stan, it was a business transaction and I was kind of suspicious initially, but I thought he was a good-looking guy. What drew me to him was, that he was "The Man," the one in charge. Once we started talking it was easy, good, natural from the beginning.

Stan and Chereace eventually married. Chereace was in debt due to a divorce and Stan was a good money manager.

Chereace: *Stan helped me to get my finances together at the beginning of our marriage. We learned more about each other and how we managed money once we cohabitated. Stan always looked at his money as a pot of money that he shared with everybody in his family. He helped his siblings by helping to provide housing for them or when he had money he was willing to share it. I was more independent. I believed that you work hard, make your own money, and get out on your own. It was my belief that your family didn't really ask you for anything. Everyone was pretty independent. Whereas how Stan grew up, his family felt if you had more money you were responsible to help them. That presented an issue in our marriage because Stan felt obligated to help them. For me, it wasn't that I didn't want to help out, but I was very mindful of not getting in God's Way. What if somebody had a repetitive problem, they would not learn a lesson if we're always giving and fixing their problem. Eventually, Stan became sneaky and went behind my back giving money to his family; which caused trust issues. I thought if you would lie about this, what else were you lying about.*

Stan: *I came from very humble beginnings. My mother raised seven kids in a three-bedroom apartment, on public assistance. She would take all of her checks, every month and not only feed her kids, but pretty much the whole neighborhood and by the fifth of* the month, she was broke. *She was a giver and gave everything away. I decided if I made it out of that environment, I had a responsibility to help my family. As much money as I made, I thought that it was my obligation to give back to my mom, siblings and extended family because I was the most successful member of the family.*

That became a huge problem down the road because it was never enough for them. I got to a point like Chereace said that I used to hide money and give money to my family under the table because I couldn't say no. Several years ago after I realized that it was affecting our marriage, I began to say no and some people even cursed me out even after saying yes for many years prior. It was a serious issue for me because I could not say no to giving money to people, especially my family. It got to a point where God had to really break me down in order for me to get it in my head that I wasn't responsible for my family's success.

So finally, I'm able to say no to people and to be totally honest with my wife about helping the family. I think we were put on this earth to help people, but there has to be a limit. As Chereace said, you can cripple people by continuing to give money to them and not have them to stand on their own two feet.

Stan: *It took a lot of prayers because one of my weaknesses is really helping people in spite of the impact on my family. It took a lot of prayers, God speaking to my heart and saying that you have to draw the line because you're getting in my way. That's what it took for me to stop it. I could not just say no, I don't have it, or no I cannot do it. When I started to do that, I would literally break out into a sweat. I felt bad when I told somebody no. It felt like I was abandoning them, but now I'm good with it.*

Chereace: *And what I will add to that from a spouse's perspective, whether it's a wife supporting a husband or husband supporting a wife, when dealing with money and family we have to exercise* patience and pray for our spouse in that particular area. I didn't come down on him or accuse him when I saw this pattern of behavior. I tried to show understanding. So I think it's important for a spouse to show compassion, understanding and seek the root cause of the issue. There's always a deeper issue and once we get to the bottom of it then we'll gain understanding. We will be able to serve and help our spouse get to a place where they need to be. As a couple, we can get on the path to doing ultimately what God wants us to do; whether it's with finances or in any area that challenges us.

Practical Advice

Chereace: Advice I would offer is to be understanding, which is the most important thing because as couples you come together in the relationship with baggage. We have this whole history of how we were brought up, our past relationships and our experiences. Instead of accusing or arguing, we can be more understanding which allows us to uncover some things about the other person and about ourselves in that process.

I think the first thing is understanding and then the other thing is communication. You should have upfront communication in key areas. When you think about the wedding vows which I love them and think they should be preserved. When we say our vows, couples should really think about what they mean, and to the extent that you can, have some ground rules around them. As a couple talks about it beforehand so you understand how you want to manage your finances. I would say understanding and then the communication is key.

Stan: I was going to say my advice was going to be communication because that's huge. But also speak the truth. One of the *things that helped me grow is to always consult the Holy Spirit first on how I should handle a situation. It was hard to really go to someone and say "Okay you're asking me for money, but you don't want my advice. You know I'm here to help you to get out of your situation. We grew up in the same household, we come from the same roots, I've been blessed in this area of finances because I've done XYZ. You keep coming to me to borrow money and you are in the same situation each and every year; operating in the same paradigm. Why don't you let me give you some advice to help you, but I'm not going to give you any more money."*

Overcoming Personality Differences Themes

Trust God

Trust each other

Communicate

Keep the faith

Seek to understand

Chapter 6

The Petition

Personality and "In Sickness and In Health"

Marriage is both rewarding and challenging. However, a sudden or chronic illness can have a catastrophic impact on a couple. One spouse taking care of the other can take a toll on the marriage. The sick or incapacitated spouse can feel like a burden and the other spouse might feel helpless. Intimacy might take a back seat in the relationship due to loss of desire, pain, or discomfort. Both spouses could end up frustrated and augmentative. You can expect each personality style to respond to this situation differently. Let's examine the potential reactions to illness in our relationships.

During the seasons of illness or chronic pain in your marriage, it requires sacrifice and restructuring roles that rarely bring recognition. As a result, some of the symptoms of this sickness could make a spouse want to "wash their hands" of the relationship.

The Sunny Sanguine

A Sanguine personality is bubbly and happy to be alive. They wake up seeing the possibilities in life. Sanguines always see the brighter side of any situation. If you come to a Sanguine with a sad situation, they will tell you the many reasons how things will work out. They will encourage you through any challenge you encounter. Sanguines will visit you and bring you chicken noodle soup. They will check up on you to make sure you have all you need to recover.

The Sickly Sanguine

As the Patient

When a Sanguine is in chronic pain or facing a debilitating illness and they are unable to enjoy life, they will usually fall into a depression.

In 2005 and 2009, I had multiple neck surgeries because of ruptured discs. I had bone taken out of my hip and fused into my neck to repair the problem. These were the most painful surgeries. During that time, my mother would call me, what seemed like, every 15 minutes to check up on me. I remember rolling my eyes and saying to my husband, "I can't talk to anyone today, please take a message." This might seem normal to other personality styles, but a Sanguine enjoys talking even when they are sick. However, this pain was so severe that I was not acting like my true self.

As the Caregiver

The Sanguine is caring and encouraging when taking care of someone who is ill or in chronic pain. They will try to make the spouse feel supported and loved by feeding, talking, and telling them that everything will be alright. The Sanguine can be annoying to the Choleric who wants to be alone and the Melancholy who craves sympathy but wallows in despair. The Phlegmatic appreciates all the attention and having to do nothing, but recover.

The Efficient/Impatient Choleric

As the Patient

The Choleric is highly productive and does not have time for illness or pain. They will grin and bear it for as long as they can. They will work through the pain or illness until they are incapable of managing it. The Choleric does not make time for doctors or doctor's appointments until it becomes necessary. Most Cholerics have a high threshold for pain and won't admit that they are having any discomfort. Choleric personalities see illness and chronic pain as a sign of weakness that prevents them from accomplishing the tasks at hand.

My hubby, who was an athlete, has bone on bone in both hips which are extremely painful, especially during the rainy season. He rarely admits he is in pain even though I see him walking with an obvious limp and a pained look on his face. When you ask him if he is in pain, he says, "a little bit" but you can see that it is worse than he lets on. Instead of having the required surgery, he is trying every natural remedy to alleviate his symptoms which have helped.

As the Caregiver

The Choleric personality will make sure you have everything you need before they go to work. They will make sure the phone, remote control, medication, water to take the medication, and food is within reach of you. They will organize people to come by and check up on you. They will expect status updates to ensure everything is taken care of. They will tell you what they think is best for you, even though you are on medical advice from a *real* doctor. Cholerics believe they know what's best for you, even without a medical degree.

When I had those multiple neck surgeries, my Choleric husband took care of me. He made sure I had everything I needed. He helped me get up and shower, fixed my breakfast, packed my meals, got my medication and stayed with me for a few days until he thought I could manage on my own with the healthcare strategy he put in place. It ran like a well-oiled machine.

The Choleric spouse becomes impatient when they believe you are not listening to their medical or healthcare advice. Remember, the Choleric is always right, at least that is what they believe. Most of the time, the Choleric is right, but there is more than one right way of doing things. Because the Choleric is efficient, their goals are to get you well as soon as possible and anything standing in the way of that annoys them.

The Nurturing/Nagging Melancholy

As the Patient:

When the Melancholy is the patient, they want peace and quiet to recover from their illness. They need to know that their spouse is taking care of them by feeding, waiting on them hand and foot and checking on them to make sure they are recovering. When you check on the well being of the Melancholy, they see it as a sign that you love and care about them. If you don't, they view it as a sign that they are not important enough to you. The Melancholy has a very long memory and will carry their hurt feelings about not being cared for to the grave.

As the Caregiver:

The Melancholy caregiver can be overbearing. They will nag you into getting you to do what they want you to do. They overreact to the initial diagnosis and potential outcome (prognosis) of their loved one's condition. They immediately see the negative in every situation, before considering the potential positive outcome. However, because of the compassionate nature of the Melancholy personality, they will nurse you back to health, making sure to follow the doctor's instructions to the letter. They will get you everything the doctor prescribed, or research homeopathy options and provide healthy foods that heal your body. They will pray for and with you until you are well and afterward, the Melancholy will nag you to do what is right and will judge you when you don't. They will let everyone know that you are not being a good patient in hopes that someone can encourage you to do what is prescribed.

The Recovering/Uninvolved Phlegmatic

As the Patient:

The Phlegmatic, much like the Melancholy, tends to assume that the worse prognosis of the source of their illness or chronic pain. To recover, the Phlegmatic will sleep as much as possible to regain their strength. They act like babies and want you to be at their beck and call. They will happily receive the care from their spouse as long as they aren't nagged into doing anything they don't want to do.

As the Caregiver:

As the caregiver, the Phlegmatic is thoughtful and kind. They will check up on their spouse to make sure they are okay. They will sit with their spouse while they recover from their illness, but don't ask them to do anything strenuous, because the Phlegmatic does not like to work. They will happily order food or find a service provider and cleaning service, but will not do any of those things themselves. The Phlegmatic doesn't like making decisions and becomes uninvolved because of the difficulty in deciding and managing their spouse's healthcare plan.

The Profession (Testimony)

Meet Andel and Celeste O who have been married for 18 years. Andel is a primary Melancholy and secondary Phlegmatic. Celeste is a primary Melancholy and secondary Phlegmatic. They met at the wedding of two of their friends. They discovered they were from the same town, had mutual friends and the day of the wedding bought the exact same card for the couple. This started a romance that brought them to the altar.

Celeste: *After six years of marriage, I was diagnosed with an aggressive form of breast cancer and that was the first time we had dealt with any kind of illness in our marriage. And then being diagnosed with that was a shock, to get that kind of diagnosis. We had just had our second child and I was diagnosed with cancer within months of having her. So, it really was a big hit to our marriage. Prior to that, I would say things were pretty smooth sailing.*

Andel: *When I heard about the diagnosis, we were in the car headed to our hometown when she got a call from her doctor letting us know. A lot of things run through your mind. I first thought I don't want to hear that. Then, I thought it was really, really bad to see that she'd have to go through that. The first thing I did was cry, although I was trying to put on a strong front.*

Celeste: *It was like the worst thing I could ever hear. But then when I saw Andel crying, it was one of the best days of my life. I was like, "You are crying?" You know, he's not a guy who cried a lot. I think I've seen him cry once in our marriage prior to that and I think that was at his grandmother's funeral or something like that. He probably doesn't remember this, but I was crying, when I saw him crying, I stopped, I said, "You really love me." I was so excited. It was really silly. I felt like we could conquer anything. I said, "This boy really loves me because he shed a tear." Of course, he cared about me, I knew that for sure. But it was just that kind of outward emotion that he was showing that really boosted me. And then we got right into the faith mode and we're believing God together that I was going to be okay.*

Andel: *We didn't have any negative people in our circle. I thank our family and friends because they were very supportive, optimistic, and they prayed for us as well. The negative experiences that we experienced most during this time came from the doctors and hospital staff. Perhaps it was because of how they approached cancer treatments and their overall mindset towards it.*

Celeste: *Exactly! The doctors were telling me it was a really aggressive form of cancer. They weren't sure if it had traveled through my system and into my body. So, they might be trained just to give you the worst-case scenario and that's what they were doing. They were definitely giving the worst-case scenario and we would just believe in God in spite of it. Our family, like Andel, said, the family was supportive and prayed for us. Any negativity I got from friends and families, I didn't even share it with Andel, because I was like, "Nope, nothing is going to turn our faith."*

Some people will say things like:

"Oh, you got diagnosed with cancer. Oh, my sister just died of cancer."

"Oh, I got a friend who just..." I'm like, "Wait, I don't want to hear that story." and they would go into further detail.

"Oh this is what was going on and this is what happened.

This is what the doctor said." "Your doctor said the same thing?"

Because, you know, they would try to confirm the diagnosis, it was almost like they would confirm that I was going to die. I know they didn't say these things intentionally.

But some people will come to me and say, "You acting all strong, but I know inside you are torn up. You don't have to be fake about it. You can cry if you need to." I was like, "Really?" Most of the time I didn't even mention it to Andel. It's wasn't worth the conversation. I will say this, Andel was absolutely amazing. The cancer experience really brought us together in a positive way. Sometimes when people go through challenges, it can make the couple grow apart. But to me, Andel was the most amazing Godsend husband ever.

Practical Advice

Celeste: *The advice I would give to other couples facing similar health issues, is that you have to keep God at the center of your life and situation. Sometimes people say, "Okay, but I really need you to hear the real way to do this." That is the real way to do it. God has to be the center. We got that diagnosis, six years into our marriage and it was a two-year process. We committed ourselves to fast every week together, even throughout our engagement. And then through the first six years of our marriage, we fasted every week together. It's important to dedicate time to God. I really believe the seeds that we planted those six years before I got the diagnosis and were reaping the fruits of it while we were going through this health concern.*

I really think the key is that we committed ourselves to God first and then, of course, committed ourselves in our marriage. But if someone's going through that challenge and you didn't commit yourself to God first and you say to yourself, "Well now I can't go backward," I say you can, do it now. You can put your health before the Lord believing nothing is impossible with Him. Come together, pray with your spouse, pray your way through it and let God give you the grace to go through it. That's the only thing that kept us. Considering I'm Melancholy, Andel is also Melancholy we can easily focus on the negative before we see the positive. It was only God's grace that kept us through the entire process. It was Him.

Andel: *I would say the advice I would offer is to support each other. Hold each other down, make plans with each other. Also, understand whoever is going through the illness, it is affecting the other person as well. Make sure you are doing all you can do for each other. Try to make life as easy as possible. Little things, weren't even worth getting mad about when we were* *dealing with the main issue that was in front of us. Be on the same page and deal with it together.*

Overcoming Personality Differences Themes

Trust God/Be Christ-centered

Keep the faith

Drown out the noise

Support each other

The next couple I want you to meet is Vince and Joy B who have been married for 26 years. Vince is a primary Sanguine, secondary Choleric and Joy is a primary Melancholy and secondary Phlegmatic. Joy and Vince met in college and there was an instantaneous connection. They dated, fell in love and got married.

Joy: *I was diagnosed in 2008 with Multiple Sclerosis (MS) and I also was diagnosed with chronic migraines. The MS whirlwind interrupted and challenged our communication, sex life, and daily routine in and outside of the household. It really challenged us.*

As a Melancholy, who strives for perfection, I could not do things perfectly with the MS. It really disrupted the perfect flow that I had going on in my household. And then as a Melancholy, I was severely challenged to come out of a dark place, but it was necessary if I was going to survive MS and live above the limitations. It was easy for me to see and think about all the things that I had lost and how difficult life was as a result of MS.

It was actually more comfortable for me to sit and wallow in despair than to actually fight my way out. I couldn't see my value outside of my physical abilities. This impacted my interaction with Vince because I couldn't see what I brought to the relationship, and didn't see the value in anything or anybody else.

Note: Melancholy personality styles are prone to depression and get stuck in a self-deprecating, negative thought process.

> *And so yeah, so that made it difficult for me to even see the changes that my husband had made, he was supporting me and taking care of me. It was difficult for me to see that because I was very consumed and overthinking and deeply thinking about what was happening and what was taking place in my life. The Choleric side of me was extremely challenged because Cholerics are natural-born leaders. We're natural-born fighters and not fighters in a bad way, but just that we remove obstacles out of our way to be successful. And as I was fighting through the MS and whatever was happening with my body, it was difficult for me to come out of fight mode and to interact positively with my husband. So when he entered the room, because I'm in fight mode when he entered in happy, I couldn't handle him being happy because I was in pain. Why are you coming in here happy? It was difficult for me to come out of fight conquer so our conversations, you know, our interaction daily it was just fiercely interrupted with that.*

Vince: *Well, you know the changes that were most notable were really physical. You know, it's heartbreaking watching her body break down, her inability to be able to take care of some of her basic needs. Joy was the administrator and Chief Operating Officer of our family and I mean she made us run well. Therefore, to lose her like that was devastating because Joy was the reason my life had joy.*

Practical Advice

Vince: *Well, the first thing I would say is don't give up hope. Just because there's a diagnosis doesn't mean there isn't life after* the diagnosis. We struggled a lot because we didn't know what life would be like after the diagnosis. I was letting my mind go crazy for a while thinking I was going to be a widower. I was clinging to Joy and probably made some decisions I shouldn't have made because I didn't know how much time I had with her. So you can only imagine when somebody's thinking short-term how that can cause some depression. The first thing is don't give up hope, there is a way to live. Then understand that you can learn to make the necessary adjustments. Get some help from support groups and educate yourself about the disease. We understood if Joy was busy one day, then the next day she may be tired, and she may not be able to have back-to-back busy days. Understand that God wouldn't allow it in your life if he didn't equip you to handle it.

You know, I understand everybody is not faith-based, but I'll tell you one thing, knowing that God has equipped me and giving me the gifts that he's given me is for a purpose, has really helped to make it through this time.

Joy: One of the things that really helped us to overcome was to give grace to ourselves. And grace is when you recognize that your spouse knows how to do something, but when they make mistakes, you don't judge or penalize them for it. There was a season when Vince and I, because of a breakdown in communication, stopped telling me about problems that were occurring in the household because the stress of it triggered my MS. We had to rebuild healthy communication and give each other the grace to make mistakes. I would encourage couples to extend grace to each other.

I love the closing vow which states, according to God's holy ordinance I pledge myself to you. The final thing I would say is to stay faithful, not based on what you're getting or what you're not getting from your spouse, but stay faithful because it pleases God. It's a commitment you made before God. And *we've been very blessed and very fortunate that 26 years later, we are still together.*

Overcoming Personality Differences Themes

Trust God

Show compassion

Keep the faith

Seek to understand

Chapter 7

The Practice

Personality and "To Love and To Cherish"

To love and to cherish is an easy vow to recite because you are in the love bubble on your wedding day. To love and to cherish means to love your spouse unconditionally and show them you appreciate them. The problem with this vow is that we fail to recognize that we are not our spouse and our spouse is not us. We appreciate our differences in the beginning, but then the very thing we love about our spouse, in the beginning, is the thing we hate the most about them when we are not getting along. For instance, one thing that I love about my husband is his sense of humor, but when we argued he would make jokes to deflect away from the issues. When I wanted a serious conversation, I did not find anything funny about his jokes.

What does "To love and to cherish" vow mean and how does it relate to the personalities?

The Affectionate Sanguine

The Sanguine personality loves love. They love the courting process and spending time together. Sanguines love intimate time with their spouse because they love physical touch and feeling connected. Sanguines love taking trips, entertaining friends and family, double-dating and going out for any reason where fun is involved. As you might have noticed, this Sanguine mentioned love six times within this small paragraph. Therefore, it is easy for the Sanguine to connect with the wedding vow "To love and to cherish." Sanguines also put their spouses and children on pedestals.

The Smothering Sanguine

Sanguines show love and affection all the time because affection is one of their emotional needs. They make some people uncomfortable with their public displays of affection (PDA). They are constantly saying "I love you" as if they don't say it, it will mean something has changed. The Sanguine can be smothering in the relationship. They want to be with their spouse all the time and give them little room to breathe. I believe they primarily wait to get married so that they will have a permanent plus one.

The Committed Choleric

To the Choleric, love means loyalty and cherish means to adore them. If the Choleric does not have their spouse's loyalty, they will feel unloved and disrespected. When the Choleric makes a commitment to marry, they make sure their spouse is the one because they intend to stay married forever. The Choleric does not waste time with someone who cannot see the vision and is not on board with it. The Choleric sees marriage as an opportunity to become a power couple. Marriage for the Choleric is as much about love as it is about establishing and running an empire.

The Curt Choleric

When the Choleric speaks on any topic, they sound harsh, even when they don't mean to and therefore are easily misunderstood. Every discussion sounds like an argument, mainly because Cholerics have to win every debate even if the person they are talking to will be wounded by the exchange. The spouse, in turn, feels as though every discussion is like showing up for battle. Even when the Choleric is wrong, they will spin the story to make sure they end up on top of a debate. The spouse finds it difficult to open up to the Choleric due to their hostile demeanor and style of communication.

The Serious-Minded Melancholy

The Melancholy personality style is serious about their commitment to marriage and will seek to learn as much about their potential spouse through a series of in-depth conversations. Because the Melancholy is always seeking an ideal mate, they will leave no stone unturned until they find them. They show their love by sharing intimate details of their past with their spouses.

The Critical Melancholy

A Melancholy personality has a hard time trusting people and if they find anything out about their spouse, they become very critical of them. When they fall in love it is with careful thought and consideration. They will cherish their spouses when they prove they can emotionally support and financially care for them. Because the Melancholy seeks an ideal mate, if at any time they decide the spouse is not doing everything that was promised during the courting period, they will seek to find someone who will.

The Supportive Phlegmatic

The Phlegmatic is content in almost every situation they are in, except when strife or stress is introduced in the marriage. They show love by offering support of their spouse's dreams, during external relationship challenges, trials, and tribulations. Going on romantic dinners or sharing their hearts with each other, which is difficult for the Phlegmatic, are the subtle things that a Phlegmatic does that makes the spouse feel loved and cherished. The Phlegmatic's tone and non-threatening demeanor demonstrate love to their spouse. When the Phlegmatic gives into the spouse's demands, they believe they are cherishing them.

The Sarcastic Phlegmatic

The Phlegmatic uses sarcasm to hide their true feelings or to state them in a non-threatening way. However, sarcasm is defined as "a sharp and often satirical utterance designed to cut or give pain." The "To love and To Cherish" vow gets trampled because of the sarcastic nature of a Phlegmatic. The nonchalant attitude of the Phlegmatic coupled with sarcasm makes the spouse feel unloved and uncherished.

The Profession (Testimony)

Meet Jon and Mary Y. who has been married for 7 years? John is a primary Phlegmatic and secondary Melancholy and Mary is a primary Melancholy and secondary Phlegmatic. Jon and Mary met on a dating app and after a courting period of 2½ years, got engaged and married 6 months later.

Mary: *One of my prayers for my future spouse, before I ever even met Jon, was I wanted to know that he loves me and cherishes me. And I wanted him to know that I loved him and cherished him as well. That was something I frequently prayed. I did not want to wonder whether he really loved me and I didn't love him and vice versa. So, I guess, being that detailed and precise in prayer is one of the characteristics of a Melancholy.*

Mary: When we had intense fellowship (Conflict), my preference was to address it right away and not let it fester. I didn't want to let the sun go down before coming to peace about an issue because if it lasted too long it would make the problem worse. There were a few times when my husband was upset and didn't want to talk. He wanted to be quiet and not address the issue. I remember one time that it was almost midnight, I would just sit down next to him and say are you going upstairs, I'm going to bed. I'd ask are you going to bed? He'd say, "No, I'm not going to bed I'm staying down here." Then I said, "Oh okay, well I'm staying down here too." I would sit down next to him until we were at peace. We had to make peace before we go to bed.

Jon: It is my nature to go somewhere and calm down because if I spoke too soon, it might not come outright. That is my style, that's what I like to do, but she wouldn't let me. Well, I remember once we had an argument over the phone. And to be honest with you, I have no idea what we were fighting about, but this is an example of me needing to get away and just calm down first. We were having a discussion, I had sent her a text and she didn't like what I said in the text. And so she called me and I'm thinking, what's wrong? What did I say? Now we're going back and forth. And at one point, she said to me, "you need to listen, I'm trying to make a point." And I said I don't think you have a point. By that time, I was so frustrated because I didn't understand why she was upset. Her response was "she felt that was like a slap." And I said it was not, and she was like yes it was, we just went around and around about the same thing. I don't remember what the argument was about, but this is why I like to be by myself and calm down first. Because this way I'm not likely to say something that I'm going to regret or have to apologize for it later.

Practical Advice

Mary: *The advice I would offer is to learn to forgive readily. Imitate how God forgives us. Forgiveness on our terms, conditionally, does not work, does not produce fruit. That's a motivator for me; I'm able to release forgiveness because that's what I want. I want that kind of forgiveness.*

Jon: *Well, I think first of all; you have to recognize that you're in a covenant relationship with God first. Then, of course, it's with your partner and because you're trying to honor God in all that you do, you're going to honor your partner in the process.*

Overcoming Personality Differences Themes

Trust God

Show compassion

Seek to understand

Chapter 8
The Plea

Personality and "Until Death Do Us Part"

"Until death do us part" literally means we stay married until one of us dies. This is the goal of all marriages or it should be. If not, what would be the point of getting married if we think it won't last? Most couples develop short and long-term marriage plans for their lives together. However, what happens when a couple plans to grow old together and one of them gets sick and eventually dies? How does the other spouse reconcile the pain of this tragic loss and move on towards a new season in their life...being a widow or widower? The uncertainty of a future without one's spouse can be frightening. This chapter serves to outline how each personality style tends to view and handle the loss of their spouse.

If a person is operating in their personality strengths their true personality will emerge during the grieving process. If not, then the surviving spouse could become self-destructive. Let's examine how each of "The Personalities" processes grief and how they overcome it by the grace of God.

The Sunny Sanguine

The Sanguine personality is an upbeat personality and does not like to be sad or to see anyone upset or grieving. They prefer to laugh, smile, and enjoy life to the fullest and they want that for others as well. Therefore, they try to avoid dealing with sadness or grief at all costs. The Sanguine is very supportive to someone who is going through a challenging time. However, the Sanguine is very emotional and wear their feelings on their sleeve. They will try to see the bright side of every situation, even a loss. When a Sanguine is grieving they will spend their time shopping and socializing to numb or avoid the pain. They can easily become social drinkers and addicted to food, fun, and relationships to cope with their sadness. When a Sanguine becomes anti-social; disinterested in going out, entertaining company, or talking to anyone, this is a signal that they are probably falling into a depressed state.

The Take-Charge Choleric

The Choleric personality is a decisive leader who exercises every opportunity to fix problems. When a Choleric is grieving they tend to take charge and handle all the funeral arrangements. A Choleric person uses productivity as a way to avoid dealing with pain and loss. The Choleric personality does not want to be upset for long because they see it as counterproductive, therefore coming to terms quickly with loss is imperative. However, as I always say, "pay me now, or pay me later." If you do not deal with your grief, it will deal with you. The Choleric personality processes their grief by throwing themselves into their work, engaging in physical activity, or becoming more controlling. When the Choleric feels out of control, they will become depressed.

The Thoughtful Melancholy

A Melancholy personality is a compassionate person who cares deeply for their family and friends. They tend to make long-range plans and therefore are devastated at the loss of a spouse. The Melancholy requires order, especially when under stress. When the Melancholy grieves, they typically organize their home and make sure all the details of the funeral are addressed. The Melancholy can easily fall into a depression and relive the details of the loss repeatedly. Processing pain for a Melancholy is challenging because they must learn to stop replaying all the negative experiences and feelings.

The Caring Phlegmatic

The Phlegmatic personality is laid-back, friendly and loyal mate. They seek peace and harmony in all relationships and environments. They are quiet and unassuming which makes them hard to read. It is difficult to determine when a Phlegmatic personality is grieving because they do not show emotion easily. They also do not like to talk about their feelings because it is hard for them to be vulnerable. The Phlegmatic personality prefers to live a stress-free, easy lifestyle. When grieving, the Phlegmatic tends to be composed and handles their emotions privately. Some people might believe that they are fine, but in reality, they are hurting inside.

To give you a sense of the personalities in the face of a tragic loss, I interviewed some spouses who suffered the loss of their mate. I think their insights will be beneficial to others who have suffered the same type of loss.

The Profession (Testimony)

Franklin and Stephanie

Meet Franklin and Stephanie D. They are both Phlegmatic/Melancholy and that means they have a lot in common. This type of couple tends to be easygoing, peaceful and enjoys quiet time. People who possess the Phlegmatic personality style tend to stay married until death because divorce is challenging and stressful for the Phlegmatic and they avoid stressful situations like the plague.

Franklin and Stephanie met in their youth and built a friendship that turned into love. When they were forced to deal with her unexpected illness, it put their faith to the test.

"My wife and I were married for just under 10 years, but last year my wife was diagnosed with metastatic end-stage cancer. Prior to that diagnosis, we had no knowledge of her condition. But in retrospect, we could see that she was sick for some time. Everything happened so fast and it caught us off guard. So, it was a really tough situation for us. My wife never went to the doctor. For as long as I've known her, I've never known her to attend any type of doctor's visit, even regular women's checkups. But on June 14, 2018, I came home from work and she told me that she thought she was going to go to the emergency room in the morning because she was experiencing shortness of breath. As I said, my wife didn't go to the doctor for anything. So, when she told me that she wanted to go, I suspected that something was really wrong. At that point, she thought that it was bronchitis. She said, as a child, she had experienced that before, so she figured the symptoms were the same. But when she said she was going, I knew this wasn't normal, so I said, I'm going with her.

So that Friday, June 15, 2018, we went to the emergency room; they ran their tests, their X-rays, and all that stuff. And of course, we were expecting them to confirm the diagnosis as bronchitis. But they told us that they spotted two lesions on her liver that resembled cancer cells. They didn't let us know the severity of it. So, they kept her in the emergency room overnight because they wanted to run more tests. The next day they set up an appointment to visit an oncologist. That was scheduled for June 22, 2018.

*On June 22, 2018, we went to Roswell Cancer Institute. And the oncologist called us in the room; she sat us down and said, "I don't know if anybody's informed you guys of the severity of the situation." She goes on to say, "your wife has cancer. She has metastatic end-stage cancer." Then she said, "**it's a strong possibility that she could be dead in 7 days.**" Seven days from June 22, 2018, would be June 29, 2018; but the total span of time was actually from June 15, 2018, to August 6, 2018,...just 52 days and she was gone.*

Franklin, as a Phlegmatic, is loyal, kind, and supportive. He stayed by his wife's side until death. As a Melancholy, he trusted and believed God would heal Stephanie. When that did not happen, it caused Franklin to question his faith and the mere existence of God.

> *"I've never experienced anything like that before. The way I describe it was a place of complete darkness. As if I was in a room with no windows or doors and somebody walked in and turned off the light because nothing made sense. Everything in my life was questioned, and I even questioned God; I questioned His motive. If I'm honest, I had a period where I, maybe, questioned His existence because I felt like, "You said, I can trust God with everything." I stand on God, I seek Him for everything and when I'm believing His word for faith or that she's going to get up and she doesn't, then I think it's only natural to say, okay, is this real or could this be wrong? Could I have been wrong? But grief is a bear, it's a dark place. When my wife died, nothing made sense. There were things that we were aspiring to and we were trying to attain. Things that we were seeking God for; that we believed that God spoke to us about, and He was leading us to, that hadn't come to fruition and I got to the place where I was kind of angry. I said God, you promised us this. And then You take her from me, and it still hasn't happened. So, was my whole life a lie? Was everything that I thought you were saying to me, a lie? Was I just totally off in my faith? You know, it's a dark place and we're approaching a year, but I'm still dealing with some of the questions.*

However, in his deep despair, he was holding tight to the promises of God. A Phlegmatic is sure that God loves them and will do right by them. I am sure this gave Franklin peace of mind. Also, as a Melancholy he praised God by worshipping Him until he was able to come out of this dark place. Stephanie was healed on the other side of Jordan (Heaven) and leaves an amazing legacy. A husband, son, family, and friends who love her deeply.

I'm in a much better place now, I'm not questioning God's existence. I'm over that. I understand and I believe, I totally believe that God is good, that all of His dealings with us are good. I totally believe that God is faithful. I have no desire to turn my back on Him at all. If anything, this is making me want to draw closer to Him.

I asked Franklin what advice would he give to a spouse who has experienced a devastating loss like this and he said:

Personally, for me and not to sound churchy if you will, but what helps me to this day to get out of those slums or those dark places is to worship. I mean not to take anything from the word because the word is the word, it's powerful, it produces, but with me, I see myself — well I know that I overcome that when I worship. God has called me to worship and I'm starting to see now that it had to do with this situation. God knew that this was going to happen and for me, it was going to take worship to get me out of it.

There have been times where I literally couldn't get off the floor. I would hit the ground and couldn't move from the weight of this. And I would just have to force myself. I wouldn't feel goosebumps. I wouldn't get this majestic feeling. I would have to literally force myself to just start praising God. But I think Karen, it always pulled me up.

As soon as I start to worship, it's like His presence is right there. Like He's never been so close. It's funny because I used to hear stuff like this all the time. I guess I never really thought much about it. But then once you experience it, it's like God really is faithful, you know, like He really is close to those that are of a broken spirit and you know, I always tell people that if I didn't know God, if I hadn't had an experience with the Love of God, if I hadn't had a relationship with God when this happened, this would have destroyed me.

Practical Advice

My advice to anybody and everybody, I don't care if you're an atheist, I don't care if you are a Christian, grief is a giant. Get close to God, draw close to God, because when I say God is faithful, Sister Karen He is faithful. Chad Delaney says, "Lord, it was You pulling me through." For me, I don't know where other people may draw strength from, but God is definitely pulling me through this. Nobody else. Nothing else. I mean there are a couple of things that I tried to turn to, for me it didn't work. But like I said, when I draw close to God, I see myself moving forward, things get a little bit clearer, it gets a little bit brighter for me. So, my advice to everybody is to look to God because He really can help, and He really will help get you through this.

Overcoming Personality Differences Themes

Trust God

Walk by faith

Worship God

Chapter 9

The Practice

Overcoming Personality Differences

After understanding the personalities and marriage vows, what's next? You need practical steps to stay connected to each other, spend time in prayer and develop spiritual warfare strategies, practice forgiveness, demonstrate compassion and consideration, strengthen communication, and date-time ideas. Every personality style needs these tools to help overcome personality differences and keep the marriage strong and healthy.

Prayer and Devotion Time

Scripture: *"But seek first the kingdom of God and His righteousness, and all these things shall be added to you".* Matthew 6:33

God should be at the center of your relationship because the more you grow closer to God the more you grow closer to each other. Spending time with God is critical to your spiritual growth and provides Godly wisdom on how to navigate your marriage.

Sanguine personalities are always talking to God, but they don't consider it devotional time. When we talk to God, it is called prayer. Sanguines need to make sure they are listening to the voice of God and not just talking.

TIP: Create a space to spend quiet time with God, blocking out distractions and noise.

Choleric personalities need to carve out time from their busy schedules so they can spend some time with God. They have a relationship with God but will try to tell God what to do. Remember the Choleric is always right, at least they think so.

TIP: The Choleric needs to humble themselves and make God the priority. Don't be afraid to surrender your daily activities to God, He will not steer you wrong. The way you can easily spend time with God is to put Him on your agenda. Use your smart device to schedule devotion time with God.

Melancholy spouses will carve out time for God with bible study and devotion time. Melancholies if not careful will beat their spouse over the head with scripture.

TIP: Be careful not to make your devotion time a god. God wants a relationship with you that requires you to interact on a human level without judgment.

Phlegmatics believe that God is their friend and wants the best for them. However, the Phlegmatic will take God's love for them for granted and not spend time with Him. Phlegmatics need to commit to their relationship by studying the word daily.

TIP: Since the Phlegmatic needs easy and simple methods to study the word, use a bible app that will text you or email you daily.

Strengthen Communication

Scripture: *For by your words you will be justified, and by your words, you will be condemned." Matthew 12:37 (NASB)*

Healthy communication is important in any relationship, but especially in a marriage. The words we speak to our spouse can uplift or destroy the marriage. We need to know that we will be judged by the things we say.

Sanguine personalities need to exercise restraint in how they speak to their spouse, especially when they are angry. Since the Bible states in Proverbs 10:19, *"In the multitude of words sin is not lacking, but he who restrains his lips is wise."* Therefore, talking too much leads to sin.

TIP: Sanguines need to step away from a hurtful situation before they make a comment they can't take back. If they cannot exit the conversation, they need to count to 20 before speaking.

Cholerics are abrasive in their communication whether angry or not. They tend to hurt their spouses' feelings without even noticing it.

TIP: Watch your spouse's body language which will give you clues as to whether they are negatively affected by your conversation. Adjust your tone and comments appropriately.

Melancholies tell the truth, but not always in love. The Melancholy's desire to be honest trump their ability to communicate with compassion and consideration.

TIP: Consider the impact of what you are saying to your spouse and see if there is a better way to say it.

Phlegmatics are sarcastic and blunt in how they communicate. They use sarcasm as a way to confront an issue in a non-threatening way. Sarcasm can be as hurtful as yelling at your spouse.

TIP: Be honest with your spouse, but speak in a caring way. Think about how your spouse will feel and adjust your comments.

Practice Forgiveness

> **Scripture:** *"And if he sins against you seven times in a day, and seven times in a day returns to you, saying, 'I repent,' you shall forgive him." Luke 17:4*

As previously stated, forgiveness is for you and does not let the other person off the hook. It lets you off the hook. Forgiveness requires humility, grace, and a desire to please God. You must want to please God more than harbor hurt feelings. One of my favorite quotes by Marianne Williamson is "Unforgiveness is like drinking poison yourself and waiting for the other person to die," So that phrase is very profound because we think if we stay mad, we are teaching our spouse a lesson, but we are only hurting ourselves.

Sanguines get angry very quickly and then they can get over it and move on as though it never happened. Sanguines will forgive their spouse because they don't want drama in the relationship.

If you hurt a Choleric, they seek revenge and will let you know they are coming after you. They harbor resentment until they feel vindicated.

Melancholies seek revenge, but they revel in the fact that you don't know that it was them who got you back. Phlegmatics appear as though they are over a situation, but they will harbor anger and overreact after a long buildup of hurtful situations.

TIPS:

- ▶ Seek to understand vs being understood
- ▶ Extend grace by not being judgmental towards each other
- ▶ Humble yourself and admit when you are wrong
- ▶ Ask your spouse for forgiveness
- ▶ Forgive yourself

Showing Compassion and Consideration

Scripture: *"But the fruit of the Spirit is love, joy, peace, longsuffering, kindness, goodness, faithfulness..." Galatians 5:22*

Showing compassion and consideration for one's spouse requires humility and selflessness. Each of the personality styles is capable of demonstrating their abilities to have (strength) or lack (weakness) compassion and/or consideration for their mate.

Sanguines are too focused on themselves to demonstrate or notice that their spouse may need emotional support from them. The Sanguine's spouse needs you to ask about what is going on with them, be quiet and listen.

A Choleric's tone alone causes their spouse to believe they are not interested in what they are going through. The Choleric will attempt to fix the issue, but not listen to what their spouse really needs. Your spouse does not always need you to fix their issue. Sometimes they just want you to listen to them. If you are unsure about what your spouse needs, ask and listen to them.

Melancholies are compassionate and they seek the same in return. They seek to be understood by their spouses. The Melancholy's decision to be compassionate to their spouse or not is based on their spouse's behaviors and attitude towards them.

Staying Connected/Dating Your Spouse

Date time helps with rekindling that spark between you. Your date time should be deliberate. The time you share should be filled with kindness, love, and respect. You can plan your "Date Time" in the morning, afternoon, or at night; it's good to mix it up a bit. The most important thing is to make a commitment to spend quality time together...no excuses. Use your time to connect, to reconnect, to live in the present, to laugh about the past and to grow your future love. Make this time about one another.

Sanguines need to have fun and excitement, but that does not have to break the bank. The most important thing to the Sanguine is the time spent with their spouse. A date-time idea might be to watch a funny movie (at home or in the theater). If you decide to watch a movie at home, be sure to set the mood with food, lighting, etc.

TIP: Make the date about spending time with the Sanguine spouse. If you are Sanguine, put your spouse's desires first.

Cholerics are achievers and they need to have a tight schedule. Therefore, the Choleric becomes annoyed at last-minute schedule changes, so it is important to book time well in advance and stick to the schedule. If the spouse is also a Choleric, they need to be flexible with their spouse if an unexpected change occurs. Because Cholerics are fast thinkers, you can easily shuffle the schedule to accommodate the change.

TIP: Cholerics need their spouse to be willing to go on an unconventional date like a daytime, morning or late-night rendezvous. Sometimes a date is as simple as running errands together. Cholerics like exciting or physical dates, for instance, rock climbing, working out in the gym or sporting events. Don't bother taking them to the movies unless it is exciting, because the Choleric is such a hard worker, they will fall asleep.

Melancholies lives by their schedule, therefore this personality needs advanced planning like the Choleric personality, but for different reasons. The Choleric needs to be efficient and be able to fit a lot into their schedule. The Melancholy needs to make sure they are taking into account feasibility, cost, and impact when scheduling their events. When scheduling a date for your Melancholy spouse, be sure it is what they want to do and that every consideration is made in scheduling it.

TIP: If you are the Melancholy mate relax and surrender your expectation to God and don't cast them on your mate. Melancholies like to do things that are educational, like visiting museums, watching educational movies, etc.

The Phlegmatic does not need advanced notice but may need some coaxing to get them out of the house. Once the Phlegmatic sits or lies down, they don't want to go out.

Phlegmatics are very laid back and prefer to go on low-key dates.

TIP: They like dinner dates, watching movies at home, or double dating. They don't like loud places with a lot of people. For the Phlegmatic spouse, don't pressure them to do anything outside of their comfort zone. For the Phlegmatic, don't be afraid to try new things even if it frightens you.

Appendix

Identifying Your Personality Style

Personality Profile sheet:

To determine your primary (dominant) and secondary personality styles, choose one of the four words on each row on the Personality Profile sheet that best describes you most of the time and place an X in front of it. Place an X in front of all forty sets of strengths and weaknesses. If you are having difficulty choosing a word, ask someone who knows you well for help.

Personality Profile Scoring Sheet

Once you complete the Personality Profile Sheet transfer your answers to the Personality Profile Scoring Sheet. Then tally each column's strengths and weaknesses to determine your primary and secondary personality styles. The highest number is your primary personality style and the second-highest score is your secondary one.

Personality Scoring Sheet Results

Most of us have a primary or secondary personality style.

The scores below indicate you are a primary Popular Sanguine and a secondary Powerful Choleric personality style:

Popular Sanguine	Powerful Choleric	Perfect Melancholy	Peaceful Phlegmatic
22	12	3	3

However, sometimes your score is extremely high in one personality style category, which means you only have a primary personality style, for example:

Combined Scores (Total points = 40)

Popular Sanguine	Powerful Choleric	Perfect Melancholy	Peaceful Phlegmatic
36	4	0	0

Appendix A

Personality Profile

PLACE AN X IN FRONT OF THE ONE WORD
ON EACH LINE THAT MOST OFTEN APPLIES TO YOU

Strengths

1 ___Adventurous	___Adaptable	___Animated	___Analytical
2 ___Persistent	___Playful	___Persuasive	___Peaceful
3 ___Submissive	___Self-sacrificing	___Sociable	___Strong-willed
4 ___Considerate	___Controlled	___Competitive	___Convincing
5 ___Refreshing	___Respectful	___Reserved	___Resourceful
6 ___Satisfied	___Sensitive	___Self-reliant	___Spirited
7 ___Planner	___Patient	___Positive	___Promoter
8 ___Sure	___Spontaneous	___Scheduled	___Shy
9 ___Orderly	___Obliging	___Outspoken	___Optimistic
10 ___Friendly	___Faithful	___Funny	___Forceful
11 ___Daring	___Delightful	___Diplomatic	___Detailed
12 ___Cheerful	___Consistent	___Cultured	___Confident
13 ___Idealistic	___Independent	___Inoffensive	___Inspiring
14 ___Demonstrative	___Decisive	___Dry humor	___Deep
15 ___Mediator	___Musical	___Mover	___Mixes easily
16 ___Thoughtful	___Tenacious	___Talker	___Tolerant
17 ___Listener	___Loyal	___Leader	___Lively
18 ___Contented	___Chief	___Chart maker	___Cute
19 ___Perfectionist	___Pleasant	___Productive	___Popular
20 ___Bouncy	___Bold	___Behaved	___Balanced

Weaknesses

21 ___Blank	___Bashful	___Brassy	___Bossy
22 ___Undisciplined	___Unsympathetic	___Unenthusiastic	___Unforgiving
23 ___Reticent	___Resentful	___Resistant	___Repetitious
24 ___Fussy	___Fearful	___Forgetful	___Frank
25 ___Impatient	___Insecure	___Indecisive	___Interrupts
26 ___Unpopular	___Uninvolved	___Unpredictable	___Unaffectionate
27 ___Headstrong	___Haphazard	___Hard to please	___Hesitant
28 ___Plan	___Pessimistic	___Proud	___Permissive
29 ___Angered easily	___Aimless	___Argumentative	___Alienated
30 ___Naive	___Negative attitude	___Nervy	___Nonchalant
31 ___Worrier	___Withdrawn	___Workaholic	___Wants credit
32 ___Too Sensitive	___Tactless	___Timid	___Talkative
33 ___Doubtful	___Disorganized	___Domineering	___Depressed
34 ___Inconsistent	___Introvert	___Intolerant	___Indiffent
35 ___Messy	___Moody	___Mumbles	___Manipulative
36 ___Slow	___Stubborn	___Show-off	___Skeptical
37 ___Loner	___Lord over others	___Lazy	___Loud
38 ___Sluggish	___Suspicious	___Short-tempered	___Scatterbrained
39 ___Revengeful	___Restless	___Reluctant	___Rash
40 ___Compromising	___Critical	___Crafty	___Changeable

Appendix B

Personality Profile
Scoring Sheet

Strengths

Popular Sanguine	Powerful Choleric	Perfect Melancholy	Peaceful Phlegmatic
1 ___Animated	___Adventurous	___Analytical	___Adaptable
2 ___Playful	___Persuasive	___Persistent	___Peaceful
3 ___Sociable	___Strong-willed	___Self-sacrificing	___Submissive
4 ___Convincing	___Competitive	___Considerate	___Controlled
5 ___Refreshing	___Resourceful	___Respectful	___Reserved
6 ___Spirited	___Self-reliant	___Sensitive	___Satisfied
7 ___Positive	___Promoter	___Planner	___Patient
8 ___Spontaneous	___Sure	___Scheduled	___Shy
9 ___Optimistic	___Outspoken	___Orderly	___Obliging
10 ___Funny	___Forceful	___Faithful	___Friendly
11 ___Delightful	___Daring	___Detailed	___Diplomatic
12 ___Cheerful	___Confident	___Cultured	___Consistent
13 ___Inspiring	___Independent	___Idealistic	___Inoffensive
14 ___Demonstrative	___Decisive	___Deep	___Dry humor
15 ___Mixes easily	___Mover	___Musical	___Mediator
16 ___Talker	___Tenacious	___Thoughtful	___Tolerant
17 ___Lively	___Leader	___Loyal	___Listener
18 ___Cute	___Chief	___Chart maker	___Contented
19 ___Popular	___Productive	___Perfectionist	___Pleasant
20 ___Bouncy	___Bold	___Behaved	___Balanced

TOTAL–STRENGTHS

_____ _____ _____ _____

Weaknesses

Popular Sanguine	Powerful Choleric	Perfect Melancholy	Peaceful Phlegmatic
21 ___Brassy	___Bossy	___Bashful	___Blank
22 ___Undisciplined	___Unsympathetic	___Unforgiving	___Unenthusiastic
23 ___Repetitious	___Resistant	___Resentful	___Reticent
24 ___Forgetful	___Frank	___Fussy	___Fearful
24 ___Fussy	___Fearful	___Forgetful	___Frank
25 ___Interrupts	___Impatient	___Insecure	___Indecisive
26 ___Unpredictable	___Unaffectionate	___Unpopular	___Uninvolved

27 ___Haphazard   ___Headstrong   ___Hard to please   ___Hesitant
28 ___Permissive   ___Proud   ___Pessimistic   ___Plain
29 ___Angered easily   ___Argumentative   ___Alienated   ___Aimless
30___Naive   ___Nervy   ___Negative attitude   ___Nonchalant
31___Wants credit   ___Workaholic   ___Withdrawn   ___Worrier
32___Talkative   ___Tactless   ___Too Sensitive   ___Timid
33___Disorganized   ___Domineering   ___Depressed   ___Doubtful
34___Inconsistent   ___Intolerant   ___Introvert   ___Indiffent
35___Messy   ___Manipulative   ___Moody   ___Mumbles
36___Show-off   ___Stubborn   ___Skeptical   ___Slow
37___Loud   ___Lord over others   ___Loner   ___Lazy
38___Scatterbrained   ___Short-tempered   ___Suspicious   ___Sluggish
39___Restless   ___Rash   ___Revengeful   ___Reluctant
40___Changeable   ___Crafty   ___Critical   ___Compromising

TOTAL- WEAKNESSES

_____   _____   _____   _____

COMBINED- TOTALS

_____   _____   _____   _____

Appendix C

References

▸ Excerpt from Personality Plus for Couples by Florence Littauer, copyright © 2001. Used by permission of Revell, adivision of Baker Publishing Group.

▸ Divorce Statistics and Facts: What Affects Divorce Rates in the U.S.? (n.d.). Retrieved from https://www.wf-lawyers.com/divorce-statistics-and-facts/

Appendix D

Recommendations

Please support the contributors to this book.

- ▶ AMD Mechanical Contractors
  http://amdmechanical.com
- ▶ Dr. Celeste Owens
  http://DrCelesteOwens.com
- ▶ Stan and Chereace Richards
  http://LoveandBusiness.net
- ▶ Vince and Joy Briscoe
  Facebook.com/VinceandJoy,
  Twitter.com/VinceandJoy
- ▶ Pastor Deborah Evans
  http://victoriouslivingnow.org/